Language in Education
Theory and Practice

APPROACHES to SYLLABUS DESIGN for FOREIGN LANGUAGE TEACHING

APPROACHES to SYLLABUS DESIGN for FOREIGN LANGUAGE TEACHING

Karl Krahnke

A publication of Center for Applied Linguistics

Prepared by Clearinghouse on Languages and Linguistics

Prentice Hall Regents, Englewood Cliffs, NJ 07632

Library of Congress Cataloging-in-Publication Data

Krahnke, Karl.
  Approaches to syllabus design for foreign language
teaching.

  (Language in education ; 67)
  "A publication of Center for Applied Linguistics."
  Bibliography: p.
  1. Language and languages--Study and teaching.
2. Curriculum planning. I. ERIC Clearinghouse on
Languages and Linguistics. II. Title. III. Series.
P53.295.K73 1987   418'.007   87-1270
ISBN 0-13-043837-5

LANGUAGE IN EDUCATION: Theory and Practice 67

Office of Educational
Research and Improvement
U.S. Department of Education

This publication was prepared with funding from the Office of Educational Research and Improvement, U.S. Department of Education, under contract no. 400-86-0019. The opinions expressed in this report do not necessarily reflect the positions or policies of OERI or ED.

Editorial/Production supervision: Martha M. Masterson
Cover design: Karen Stephens
Manufacturing buyer: Margaret Rizzi

Published 1987 by Prentice-Hall, Inc.
A Division of Simon & Schuster
Englewood Cliffs, New Jersey 07632

Printed in the United States of America

10 9 8 7 6 5 4 3 2

ISBN 0-13-043837-5 01

Prentice-Hall International (UK) Limited, London
Prentice-Hall of Australia Pty. Limited, Sydney
Prentice-Hall Canada Inc., Toronto
Prentice-Hall Hispanoamericana, S.A., Mexico
Prentice-Hall of India Private Limited, New Delhi
Prentice-Hall of Japan, Inc., Tokyo
Prentice-Hall of Southeast Asia Pte. Ltd., Singapore
Editora Prentice-Hall do Brasil, Ltda., Rio de Janeiro

Contents

Language in Education: Theory and Practice

ERIC (Educational Resources Information Center) is a nationwide network of information centers, each responsible for a given educational level or field of study. ERIC is supported by the Office of Educational Research and Improvement of the U.S. Department of Education. The basic objective of ERIC is to make current developments in educational research, instruction, and personnel preparation readily accessible to educators and members of related professions.

ERIC/CLL. The ERIC Clearinghouse on Languages and Linguistics (ERIC/CLL), one of the specialized clearinghouses in the ERIC system, is operated by the Center for Applied Linguistics (CAL). ERIC/CLL is specifically responsible for the collection and dissemination of information on research in languages and linguistics and its application to language teaching and learning.

LANGUAGE IN EDUCATION: THEORY AND PRACTICE. In addition to processing information, ERIC/CLL is also involved in information synthesis and analysis. The Clearinghouse commissions recognized authorities in languages and linguistics to write analyses of the current issues in their areas of specialty. The resultant documents, intended for use by educators and researchers, are published under the series title, Language in Education: Theory and Practice. The series includes practical guides for classroom teachers and extensive state-of-the-art papers.

This publication may be purchased directly from Prentice-Hall, Inc., Book Distribution Center, Route 59 at Brook Hill Dr., West Nyack, NY 10995, telephone (201) 767-5049. It also will be announced in the ERIC monthly abstract journal *Resources in Education (RIE)* and will be available from the ERIC Document Reproduction Service, Computer Microfilm International Corp., 3900 Wheeler Ave., Alexandria, VA 22304. See *RIE* for ordering information and ED number.

For further information on the ERIC system, ERIC/CLL, and CAL/Clearinghouse publications, write to ERIC Clearinghouse on Languages and Linguistics, Center for Applied Linguistics, 1118 22nd St. NW, Washington, DC 20037.

Gina Doggett, Editor, Language in Education

1
The Place
of the Syllabus
in Language Teaching

In any case, teachers of English as a second language are on the whole more used to thinking about methodology than about syllabus design.
(Yalden, 1983, p. 17)

Among the various aspects of second or foreign language teaching, one of the most ignored has been the content of the teaching, what is generally referred to as curriculum or syllabus design. While teachers and administrators frequently speak of differences in *method,* differences in the *content* of instruction are examined much less often. While the content of language teaching has generally been discussed in terms of three types of syllabus—the structural, the situational, and, most recently, the notional/functional—six different ways to define language teaching syllabi are examined here. Each type will be defined as though it existed independently of the others, although in practice syllabus types are frequently combined. Possible applications are suggested for each type of syllabus, and each is evaluated. In addition, grounds for choosing a syllabus type are discussed, along with various ways in which syllabi can be combined and implemented in a second or foreign language teaching program.

This discussion of language teaching syllabi will concentrate on the teaching of English as a second or foreign language. This focus excludes a great amount of work in the teaching of other languages. However, extensive literature is available on the teaching of English, and all the questions arising from it can easily be generalized to the teaching of other foreign languages. In addition, this approach eliminates the need to cite examples in a variety of foreign languages. Teachers of other languages should be able to supply the necessary examples from their own fields.

The distinction between curriculum and syllabus is not a major concern here. While a distinction is frequently made in the literature, it is rarely clear. What is usually assumed is that curriculum includes syllabus, but not vice versa (see Dubin & Olshtain, 1986, p. 3, for an example of this view). A syllabus is more specific and more concrete than a curriculum, and a curriculum may contain a number of syllabi. For example, a curriculum may cover an entire school year, while a language teaching syllabus may make up only one part of the curriculum. Or the overall curriculum of a full-time intensive language teaching program may include three or more specific skill-area syllabi at any one time. A curriculum may specify only the goals (what the learners will be able to do at the end of the instruction), while the syllabus specifies the content of the lessons used to move the learners toward the goals.

Content, or what is taught, is the single aspect of syllabus design to be considered here. Content is only one element of some actual teaching syllabi that include behavioral or learning objectives for students, specifications of how the content will be taught, and how it will be evaluated. These are all valid and important concerns, but they are, again, broader questions than the questions of which definition of language will be assumed by the instruction and what choice of linguistic content will form the basis and the organization for the instruction.

The six approaches to syllabus design presented here can be characterized as differing by increasing attention to language use and decreasing attention to language form. The use/form continuum can be viewed as a scale on which to measure various actual syllabus decisions. The six types will be summarized in Chapter 2, and considered in detail in each of the following six chapters. But first, it would be useful to relate syllabus design to the broader context of language teaching.

Uncertainty about what the components or ingredients of language teaching are has resulted in a confusing discussion of *method* versus *approach* versus *syllabus,* and so on. A taxonomy of the major elements or components of language teaching is needed so that like items can be compared or contrasted. The best taxonomy of the language teaching enterprise available is by Richards and Rodgers (1982, 1986).

According to the analysis of language teaching proposed by Richards and Rodgers, "method" is the cover term for all of language teaching, from theory to practice. *Method* is divided into the three levels of (a) *approach,* (b) *design,* and (c) *procedure. Approach* is further divided into theories of language and theories of learning. *Design* is divided into syllabus design and content; roles of materials; roles of learners; and roles of teachers. *Procedure* specifies the activities that are actually used in a classroom.

Richards and Rodgers argue that all "methods" exist on all levels, although they may not be explicitly documented on all levels. The implicit assumptions about language learning made by, for example, Gattegno's (1972) method, the Silent Way, are as real as the explicit assumptions of cognitive code learning. Since language teaching can be analyzed into relatively discrete components, comparisons between methods are facilitated.

The element of method that is most relevant here is that of the syllabus on the design level. It is worthwhile to quote Richards and Rodgers at length in defining the syllabus:

> All methods of language teaching involve the use of the target language. All methods involve decisions concerning the selection of content that is to be used in the teaching program. Content concerns involve both subject matter and linguistic matter. In straightforward terms one makes de-

cisions as to what to talk about (subject matter) and how to talk about it (linguistic matter). ESP [English for special purposes] and immersion courses, for example, are necessarily subject-matter focused. Structurally-based courses are necessarily linguistically focused. Methods typically differ in what they see as the relevant language and subject matter around which language instruction should be organized and the principles they make use of in structuring and sequencing content units within a course.

(1982, p. 157)

A language teaching syllabus, then, is the linguistic and subject matter that make up the teaching. Choices range from more or less purely linguistic syllabi, where the content of instruction is the grammatical and lexical forms of the language, to the purely semantic or informational, where the content of instruction is some skill or information and only incidentally the form of the language. Methods differ from each other in many ways—in classroom procedures, roles for teachers and learners, and in theories of language and learning—but one of the more explicit ways in which they differ is in their definitions of the content of the instruction, or the design of the syllabus.

The aspect of language teaching method that is most closely related to syllabus is the theory of language that is assumed by the method. To design a syllabus is to decide *what* gets taught and in what order. For this reason, the theory of language explicitly or implicitly underlying the method will play a major role in determining what syllabus is adopted.

While there is no clear taxonomy of theories of language, the definition of communicative competence provided by Canale (1983) is the most useful for language teachers. Although many writers mistakenly consider communicative competence to be distinct from linguistic competence (e.g., Paulston, 1974), in Canale's taxonomy linguistic or grammatical competence is but one component of the overall ability to know a language and function in it. According to Canale, communicative competence (or language proficiency) can be divided into *grammatical, sociolinguistic, discourse,* and *strategic* competence.

Canale's taxonomy of language and the components of communicative competence provide a way to describe various theories of language that underlie language teaching methods and affect syllabus design. The structural or grammatical theory assumes that grammatical competence is primary or basic. A functional or semantic theory assumes that sociolinguistic competence is primary. A communicative or use-based theory of language assumes that discourse and strategic competence are primary. Certainly, the broad construct of language can be analyzed differently from the way Canale has analyzed it, but, for the present, Canale's components of communicative competence are most useful for characterizing the differences in theory of language underlying various methods.

A theory of language is not, however, the only basis for syllabus choice; theory of learning will also play an important part. For example, a teacher may accept a structural theory of language, but not accept that learners can acquire language material according to a strict grammatical sequence of presentation. While the basic view of language may be structural, the syllabus, in that case, may be more situational or even content-based. Only with the audio-lingual method in the 1960s did language teaching operate on a clearly enunciated theory of learning— behaviorism. Although they were never as clearly formulated and stated, cognitive code methods were based on a theory of learning that called for conscious recognition of the structures and patterns of language form.

More recently, Krashen (1982) proposed a theory of learning that is characterized by unconscious acquisition of language ability through exposure to appropriate language input in meaningful settings, assigning a minor role to conscious learning and formal practice.

Clearly, a syllabus based on the theory of learning espoused by cognitive code teaching would have to emphasize language forms and whatever explicit descriptive knowledge about those forms was presently available. A syllabus based on an acquisition theory of learning, however, would emphasize unanalyzed, though possibly carefully selected, experiences of the new language in an appropriate variety of discourse types.

Learner type is another variable in the choice of syllabus. Much has been said and written about types of learner in the last several decades (Birckbichler & Omaggio, 1978; Brown, 1980). A prevailing belief in language teaching is that there are numerous and distinct types of learners and learning, and that different experiences should be provided so these learners can proceed toward the same goal of communicative competence in their own manner (Krahnke & Knowles, 1984). Unfortunately, little empirical evidence supports the notion that there really are different types of language learners (see Corbett & Smith, 1984, for a relevant negative study), although experience suggests that there are. Even less evidence exists showing that all learning styles are equally effective and lead to the same end. At present, it seems most probable that there are different types of learners, and the difference between them leads more to difference in overall proficiency than it does to the same proficiency through different routes.

Learner type can, then, be considered a causal factor in syllabus choice, although no principled basis exists for doing so. Learner types can be seen in practical and observable terms, such as type of cognitive activity, life style, aspirations, employment, educational and social backgrounds, and so on. These are much more salient categories than field dependence/independence, tolerance for ambiguity, or ego permeability. The more observable characteristics allow for easier choices about syllabi than the more abstract and hypothetical constructs. Clearly, learners who intend to limit their use of a new language to very specific and narrow applications, such as taking orders in a restaurant, have quite different instructional needs from those of the immigrant with career and social aspirations. And learners with no previous experience with language in written modes, no formal education, and immediate work and residence needs require quite different instruction from students learning the new language as a school subject.

The choice of a syllabus is a major decision in

language teaching, and it should be made as consciously and with as much information as possible. There has been much confusion over the years as to what different types of content are possible in language teaching syllabi and as to whether the differences are in syllabus or method. Several distinct types of language teaching syllabus are presented in the following chapters, from the most formal to the most semantic or use-based, and the ways in which the various types can and should be implemented in various teaching situations are discussed.

This is not, however, a how-to for syllabus design, describing the process a teacher or program should go through to produce a usable document or definition of content. Instead, it describes types of product, the different kinds of content that can be included in language teaching, and some principles to be invoked in deciding what type or types to use. The process of constructing, implementing, or modifying an existing syllabus is another matter that deserves a work of its own.

2
Six Types of Language Teaching Syllabus

Each of six different types of language teaching syllabus is treated here largely as though it occurred "purely," or independently of the other types. In practice, of course, these different types rarely occur independently of each other. Almost all actual language teaching syllabi are combinations of two or more of the types defined here. On the other hand, for a given course, text, or curriculum, one type of syllabus usually dominates; that is, while other types of content may be combined with the dominant type, the majority of the content reflects one or another type of syllabus. Furthermore, the six types of syllabus are not entirely distinct from each other. The distinction between syllabi defined as skill-based and those defined as task-based, for example, may be minimal. In such cases, the distinguishing factor is often the way in which the instructional content is used in the actual teaching procedure. The six types are treated separately so that their characteristics, differences, and strengths and weaknesses can be clearly defined. There is no recommendation that language teaching adopt one or another in pure form for any purpose whatsoever.

The question of selecting, implementing, and, possibly, combining syllabi is discussed in Chapter 9. For now, brief definitions of the six types of syllabi to be examined are as follows:

1. A *structural* (or formal) syllabus is one in which the content of language teaching is a collection of the forms and structures, usually grammatical, of the language being taught. Examples of structures include: nouns, verbs, adjectives, statements, questions, complex sentences, subordinate clauses, past tense, and so on, although formal syllabi may include other aspects of language form such as pronunciation or morphology.

2. A *notional/functional* syllabus is one in which the content of the language teaching is a collection of the functions that are performed when language is used, or of the notions that language is used to express. Examples of functions include: informing, agreeing, apologizing, requesting, promising, and so on. Examples of notions include size, age, color, comparison, time, and so on.

3. A *situational* syllabus is one in which the content of language teaching is a collection of real or imaginary situations in which language occurs or is used. A situation usually involves several participants who are engaged in some activity in a specific setting. The language occurring in the situation involves a number of functions, combined into a plausible segment of discourse. The primary purpose of a situational language teaching syllabus is to teach the language that occurs in the situations. Sometimes the situations are purposely relevant to the present or future needs of the language learners, preparing them to use the new language in the kinds of situations that make up the syllabus. Examples of situations include: seeing the dentist, complaining to the landlord, buying a book at the bookstore, meeting a new student, asking directions in a new town, and so on.

4. A *skill-based* syllabus is one in which the content of the language teaching is a collection of specific abilities that may play a part in using language. Skills are things that people must be able to do to be competent in a language, relatively independently of the situation or setting in which the language use can occur. While sit-

uational syllabi group functions together into specific settings of language use, skill-based syllabi group linguistic competencies (pronunciation, vocabulary, grammar, sociolinguistic, and discourse) together into generalized types of behavior, such as listening to spoken language for the main idea, writing well-formed paragraphs, giving effective oral presentations, taking language tests, reading texts for main ideas or supporting detail, and so on. The primary purpose of skill-based instruction is to learn the specific language skill. A possible secondary purpose is to develop more general competence in the language, learning only incidentally any information that may be available while applying the language skills.

5. A *task-based* syllabus and a content-based syllabus are similar in that in both the teaching is not organized around linguistic features of the language being learned but according to some other organizing principle. In task-based instruction the content of the teaching is a series of complex and purposeful tasks that the students want or need to perform with the language they are learning. The tasks are defined as activities with a purpose other than language learning, but, as in a content-based syllabus, the performance of the tasks is approached in a way that is intended to develop second language ability. Language learning is subordinated to task performance, and language teaching occurs only as the need arises during the performance of a given task. Tasks integrate language (and other) skills in specific settings of language use. They differ from situations in that while situational teaching has the goal of teaching the specific language content that occurs in the situation—a predefined *product* —task-based teaching has the goal of teaching students to draw on resources to complete some piece of work—a *process*. The language students draw on a variety of language forms, functions, and skills, often in an individual and unpredictable way, in completing the tasks. Tasks that can be used for language learning are, generally, tasks that the learners actually have to perform in any case. Examples are applying for a job, talking with a social worker, getting housing information over the telephone,

completing bureaucratic forms, collecting information about preschools to decide which to send a child to, preparing a paper for another course, reading a textbook for another course, and so on.

6. A *content-based* syllabus is not really a language teaching syllabus at all. In content-based language teaching, the primary purpose of the instruction is to teach some content or information using the language that the students are also learning. The students are simultaneously language students and students of whatever content is being taught. The subject matter is primary, and language learning occurs incidentally to the content learning. The content teaching is not organized around the language teaching, but vice-versa. Content-based language teaching is concerned with information, while task-based language teaching is concerned with communicative and cognitive processes. An example of content-based language teaching is a science class taught in the language the students need or want to learn, possibly with linguistic adjustments to make the science more comprehensible.

In general, the six types of syllabi or instructional content are presented beginning with the one based most on language structure, and ending with the one based most on language use. If language is viewed as a relationship between form and meaning, and instruction as emphasizing one or the other side of this relationship, then the six types of syllabi can be represented as a continuum, ranging from that based most on form to that based most on meaning. Such a relationship can be represented in graphic form as in Figure 2.1.

structural	notional-functional	situational	skill-based	task-based	content-based

```
-------:----------------:-----------------:-----------------:------------:-------------:-------
```

emphasis on form   emphasis on meaning

Figure 2.1. Continuum of syllabi.

Another way of differentiating them is the degree to which they call for an analysis of the language before it is presented to the learner. In a structural syllabus, the analysis of the language and language behavior is done before the teaching, and the teaching consists of presentations of the results of the analysis to the learner. The learner, then, presumably incorporates the knowledge into behavior. In a content-based syllabus, the learner experiences the language without benefit of preanalysis on the part of the teacher or syllabus designer (although adjustments in the language being used may be made to facilitate comprehension and learning), and must carry out whatever psycholinguistic processes are necessary to develop the new language behaviors himself or herself.

Yalden (1983) lists four paradigms that reflect a spectrum of syllabus types like those that have been characterized here. They are synthetic-analytic, formal-functional, structural-contextual, and grammatical-communicative. All fall well within the extremes of the spectrum. Clearly, some instructional content is relatively removed from any real or imagined context of use, and some instructional content is identical with the language being learned.

The six archetypes presented here differ in the ways in which they relate linguistic form to meaning and use. The structural syllabus in its idealized form presents language form removed from actual occasions of use. The notional/functional syllabus attempts to relate language forms to occasions of use by presenting canonical or customary relations between form and categories of use (functions). The situational syllabus and skill-, task-, and content-based syllabi all present language forms in various types of contexts of use. The situational syllabus provides idealized settings, presenting language forms to the learner on the basis of intuition or investigation on the part of the course writer. The skill-based syllabus does it by defining types of use on the discourse level and requiring the learner to apply the skills to real or imaginary language forms. The task-based syllabus does it by defining some process or goal that the learner has to achieve in the language and requiring the learner to carry out the process or reach the goal, using naturally occurring language forms and real information to achieve it. The content-based syllabus does it by requiring the learner to acquire some knowledge through the occasion of use directly, with the acquisition of language form subordinated to the acquisition of knowledge.

All of these approaches to content have succeeded in getting language students to learn a new language, although task-based syllabi are relatively new and untested. Choosing between and among the various types of syllabus or instructional content and integrating them in a useful and effective way in an actual teaching program requires an awareness of the strengths and shortcomings of each.

In the following chapters, each of these types of content in language teaching is examined in greater detail.

3

The Structural Syllabus

The structural or grammatical syllabus is doubtless the most familiar of syllabus types. It has a long history, and a major portion of language teaching has been carried out using some form of it. The structural syllabus is based on a theory of language that assumes that the grammatical or structural aspects of language form are the most basic or useful. When functional ability, or ability to use or communicate in the new language, is a goal of instruction, the structural syllabus can be said to embrace a theory of learning that holds that functional ability arises from structural knowledge or ability.

The content of the structural syllabus is language form, primarily grammatical form, and the teaching is defined in terms of form. Although the definition of language form and the most appropriate "grammar" to use in pedagogy have long been disputed, most existing structural syllabi use some form of traditional, Latin-based, descriptive/prescriptive grammatical classification and terminology. The usual grammatical categories are the familiar ones of noun, verb, pronoun, adjective, singular, plural, present tense, past tense, and so on. The domain of structural syllabi has tended to be limited to the sentence. That is, the sentence is the largest unit of discourse that is regularly treated. A classification of sentence types usually includes semantically defined types such as statements or declaratives, questions or interrogatives, exclamations, and conditionals; and grammatically defined types such as simple, compound, and complex sentences.

A good deal of morphology can also be found in structural syllabi, such as singular and plural marking, the forms marking the tense system of the language, and special morphology such as determiners and articles, prepositions and postpositions, gender markers, and so on. Morphology also deals with vocabulary, specifically formal aspects such as prefixes and suffixes.

A key feature of the structural syllabus is that it is "synthetic" (Wilkins, 1976; Yalden, 1983). Synthetic syllabi require analyses of the language (content), such as word frequency counts, grammatical analysis, and discourse analysis. The syllabus designer uses the elements isolated as a result of the analyses to make up the content of the syllabus. In most cases these are rules, patterns, and grammatical elements, usually with guidelines for their combination and use. Because of their synthetic nature, structural syllabi assume a general theory of learning that holds that learners can synthesize the material being taught in one of at least two ways. First, the analyzed information—the rules and patterns—are available as the learner attempts to use them in linguistic communication. The learner uses the information either to generate or produce utterances or discourse, or to check the accuracy of production. Second, analyzed information is transformed from analyzed, possibly conscious knowledge, into the largely unconscious behavior that makes up language use.

There are several ways to present language structure, of course. For example, the syllabus may call for descriptive ability on the part of the students. That is, the students are expected to be able to *describe* rules or *explain* why an utterance is right or wrong. This is explicit structural knowledge. A second type of structural knowledge is reflected in recognition or judgmental ability. This is the type of structural knowledge or ability that native speakers have—the ability merely to judge whether a given form is acceptable or not, and, usually, to correct unacceptable forms. A third possible goal of structural teaching is accurate productive behavior—the learners should become able to *use* the structures being taught without necessarily being able to describe or make judgments about them. These are three quite different uses of structure in the classroom, and teaching often does not keep them clearly distinct. The first, at least, would require a very different type of instructional content than the other two. Teaching for descriptive or explanatory ability would require that the instruction include explicitly stated rules and explanations, which the other approaches might not need to include.

Structural syllabi have most frequently been associated with cognitive methods of language teaching, audiolingualism, grammar-translation methods, and several innovative methods such as the Silent Way. Some versions of cognitive theory have asserted that languages are best learned through conscious knowledge of the forms of the language and the rules for their combination. Audio-lingual methods use a behaviorist learning model to instill structural knowledge and behavior in learners. Grammar-translation methods present the grammatical forms and patterns of the language explicitly, and then call for the student to practice and apply the knowledge in translating from his or her native language to the language being learned, and vice versa. More recent cognitive methods dispense with the translation, but still call for explicit identification of the forms and structures of the language combined with application and practice focusing on the forms (Carroll, 1966; Rivers, 1981).

With structural syllabi, the problem of selecting instructional content is usually minimal. Except in the case of uncommonly taught languages, the grammatical structure of the language being taught is usually well known. Of course, especially in recent years as syntactic facts have accumulated through work in syntactic theory, many little-known aspects of the grammars of even well-known languages have been documented.

One minor problem with the selection of content is the degree of detail the instruction should be concerned with. A grammatical point can be presented in a basic or general way, with little detail and few exceptions, or it can be presented with all of its quirks and intricacies. For example, in teaching the English present perfect tense, it is not immediately obvious how much to distinguish it from the past tense in order to provide learners with useful knowledge.

While the selection of content is not a major problem, the sequencing or grading of the content is. Several criteria have been proposed for determining the order in which to present various structures and patterns in a language. Kelly (1969) provides a historical perspective, and identifies complexity ("facility"), regularity ("grammatical analysis"), and productivity, or the usefulness of the structure, as the three most frequently invoked criteria. A recent summary is provided by Canale and Swain (1980). The familiar criterion of grammatical complexity is, of course, primary, although no objective measure has ever been established, and syllabus and materials writers have had to resort to intuitive criteria or "the cumulative experience of language teachers" (Alexander, 1976, p. 91) to determine complexity and sequencing. Other criteria are communicative facility, communicative generalizability, degree of facilitation of acquisition of other structures, perceptual accessibility, and dialectal markedness. Strict sequencing of structures in language teaching syllabi is to be avoided because it leads to difficulties in applying the concepts to specific cases.

Other criteria that can be invoked in making sequencing decisions include degree of difference between the structure concerned and its equivalent in the learners' first language, the learners' communicative need for the structure, and the order in which the structure occurs in a natural acquisition sequence.

Ultimately, however, the sequencing problem is unsolved. No single criterion is used, and empirical evidence is lacking. In practice, sequencing decisions are generally based on presumed simplicity, frequency, and need. In English, for example, the simple present tense is usually presented before the more complex present continuous, and the past before the present perfect. Ordering of the present continuous and the past, however, remains variable, and principles for sequencing them relative to each other are lacking.

Yalden (1983) summarized the structural sequences used in a number of textbooks. Although she concludes that there is great similarity in their sequencing, in fact, structures such as the ones just mentioned are presented in quite varying order in different texts. Of the four sequences examined by Yalden, the future tense was presented before the present perfect in two and after it in two. The present continuous was presented much earlier than the past in one text and after the past in two.

The sequencing or grading problem is complicated by questions of learning theory, whether structures are to be mastered on initial presentation or gradually refined and expanded during repeated presentations (spiraling), and by problems of relation to and integration with other types of syllabus. These issues will be considered again in Chapter 9.

Examples of Structural Syllabi

Textbooks are not syllabi, but they frequently become syllabi and they certainly reflect what informed writers believe should be the content and order of teaching. Rather than provide an example of an imaginary structural syllabus, or of a real but unrepresentative one, the content and order of several representative ESL textbooks are provided as examples of structural syllabi.

The following partial content list is from a textbook series for beginning students of ESL that is structurally organized, although it contains some situational content. The book is *New English 900,* published in 1978 by Collier Macmillan.

This and *that*
My, your
Be, present tense
Subject pronouns
Predicate adjectives
Subject pronouns—plural
Possessive adjectives
Demonstrative pronouns
Imperatives
Negative of *be*

Third singular present tense
Simple past
Negative questions
Going to future
Could as possibility
Adjectives of comparison—
  -er, -est
Two-word verbs
Could—past of *can*
Infinitives

Tag questions
Count, noncount
Present continuous
Possessive pronouns
Past of *be*
Simple present
May, may not
Can, can't
Simple present, negative
Count and mass nouns
Frequency adverbs

Indirect object position
Will future
Would like, would rather
Must, must not
Past continuous
Embedded *wh* clauses—
   relative clauses
Reflexives
-ly adverbs
Should
If + real condition

Note that the groupings and grading tend to follow an order of difficulty and frequency of use, and that not all formally related material is presented at once. The modals, for example, are presented separately from each other, presumably in an order based on frequency or communicative need.

The second example is from *Understanding and Using English Grammar* (Azar, 1981), one of the most widely used recent ESL structural texts. The contents of the book are as follows (with some abbreviations):

Questions
    yes/no
    Wh-questions
    negative questions
    tag questions

Singular and plural
    subject-verb agreeement
    pronoun agreement
    some singular, plural usages of nouns—irregular noun plurals,
        count and noncount nouns, etc.

Verb tenses
    irregular verbs and spelling
    an overview of English verb tenses—simple, progressive, perfect,
        etc.
    using verb tenses—simple present, present progressive, etc.

The passive

Modal auxiliaries

Gerunds and infinitives

Adjective clauses
Noun clauses
Conjunctions

Adverb clauses and related structures
        time, cause, and effect
        opposition and condition

Comparison

Conditional sentences

Gerunds and infinitives (advanced)

Note that structural material is grouped in this book according to type. Obviously, this book is not intended as the sole learning source for students; otherwise, all they could do for the first unit would be to ask questions. Presumably, this is a remedial or review grammar, intended to increase students' existing knowledge.

Positive Characteristics of Structural Syllabi

Structural approaches to language teaching have come under severe criticism at many times in the history of the field (Kelly, 1969) for many obvious reasons. Nevertheless, structural syllabi, either in their pure form or in combination with other types of syllabi, remain the most common in the language teaching world. Several factors account for structural syllabi's popularity that are also reasons why structural content needs to be considered in language teaching.

One reason, frequently overlooked in recent discussions, is that structure or grammar is the most general component of communicative competence. Every utterance, if it is reasonably well formed, involves a given structure, which can be used for a variety of functions, situations, and meanings. Because form is the most generalizable aspect of language, it can be argued, it should be the basis for language course content. The fundamental nature of structure has been restated by much recent work in second language acquisition, almost all of which (see Dulay, Burt, & Krashen, 1982, for a summary) has focused on the development of structure. Dulay and Burt (1976) argue for the use of structure as an index of overall linguistic development. Thus, despite doubts about the utility of structural knowledge, the importance of structural ability in language use is recognized. The question of how easily formal knowledge transfers to functional ability remains unanswered, however.

A second reason for the popularity of structural syllabi is simple familiarity. "Grammar" is frequently expected in a language class and usually constitutes familiar content. The grammar of a language may be complex, but the basic outlines are generally well known and make up a relatively finite body of knowledge. If a language course promises to teach the basic grammar of the language, prospective learners are fairly sure of what to expect.

A third feature of structural syllabi is that their content is relatively easy to describe. *Noun, verb, imperative, plural,* and *gerund* are terms that are generally shared within the language profession, and there is general agreement about what they mean. This is certainly more true of structure than it is of, say, the functions of language, where the definitions are often unfamiliar and frequently not agreed on by the "experts." More important, grammatical concepts are simply better defined than functional ones: A past tense is a clearer concept than an invitation or a directive.

A fourth reason why structural syllabi are frequently used is that structural knowledge is the most measurable of the components of communicative competence. Because of the relative finiteness of structural knowledge and its relatively clear definition, measurement tasks are easily prepared to determine how much students have or have not learned. The grammar test is a familiar task, and its presence on almost any type of language evaluation is evidence of its ease of use. Also, it is easier to make right-or-wrong decisions about the structural aspects of learners' language than about any other aspect. Since much of language instruction takes place in contexts in which learners' knowledge is measured, either to rank students or to measure their progress, the choice of a structural basis for instruction and evaluation often seems natural.

Fifth, while structural knowledge does not seem to be used directly by learners (see Ellis, 1986, for a thorough discussion), some evidence (Higgs & Clifford, 1982) suggests that it can prevent later fossilization or cessation of learning. Basing their conclusions on non-experimental longitudinal observations and an analysis of the prior experience of students who succeed and those who fail to progress past an intermediate stage of language learning, Higgs and Clifford state that the only factor that clearly differentiates the successful from the unsuccessful learner is prior instruction in the structure of the language. Generally, students who ultimately achieved high proficiency in a new language were students who had earlier received instruction in the form of the language. Students who fossilized or were not able to progress beyond a high intermediate stage were those who had acquired the language without benefit of much formal instruction. Much more research needs to be done to investigate and validate Higgs and Clifford's suggestion, however.

Sixth, according to the prevailing theory of language acquisition, Krashen's acquisition or "Monitor Theory" (Krashen, 1982, 1985), structural knowledge can play a limited but well-defined role in language use by serving as the basis for the learner to Monitor, or check on the accuracy of production and self-correct according to known rules when time and the attention of the language user allow for it. These conditions are met only on discrete-point language tests and, to some degree, in the editing of writing. Monitoring is also limited to the use of relatively easy rules, and there is some evidence (Tarone, 1986) that the attempt to Monitor using complex rules actually decreases the accuracy of language production. According to Krashen's theory, however, Monitoring, within the limitations he proposes for it, does play a useful role in second language performance, and Krashen recommends the teaching of structural knowledge so that second language learners can use such knowledge under the conditions that allow for it.

Seventh, instruction in language structure offers a

basis for teachers or others to provide learners with feedback on the accuracy of their production. Learners' errors are corrected with specific reference to previous instruction in accurate forms or to explanations or rules. This factor is of doubtful value because extensive evidence has demonstrated that such overt error correction has no effect on accuracy. Nevertheless, error correction is a widely accepted and practiced technique for dealing with learners' errors, and many teaching curricula call for it.

Eighth, structural syllabi are naturally value- and culture-free. They can be taught independently of cultural values in instructional settings where the language itself may be desired, but not the social and cultural values that are associated with it. This is becoming increasingly true in some developing countries, where major world languages such as English are needed, but for political, social, or religious reasons, authorities do not want the social and cultural values of England, the United States, or other English-speaking countries to be imported along with the language.

Negative Characteristics of Structural Syllabi

Several notorious weaknesses are associated with structural syllabi. The most important of these is the usability, applicability, or transferability of structural knowledge. Structural knowledge may be teachable, and there is some evidence that it is learnable, but there is almost no evidence that it affects behavior in language use to any great degree. Studies of the relationship of teaching of language form to writing ability in the learners' first language, for example, have shown that it has no measurable effect on any aspect of their writing ability (Hartwell, 1985). The studies on the order of acquisition of certain basic structures in languages, measured by appearance in actual language use, show little or no relation to the order in which they are usually taught or the order in which the studies' subjects were taught. Instruction in structure, therefore, does not seem to transfer to behavior very well or easily, if at all (see Ellis, 1986, for a detailed treatment of this question).

Although the real and apparent successes of structure-based teaching cannot be fully described here, several points can be made. First, many students do "learn" structural matter, and they can demonstrate their knowledge on certain types of tests, but this knowledge does not seem to manifest itself during unmonitored language use. Thus the knowledge is learnable, but the degree to which it is usable is questionable. Second, while instruction in form may have few *direct* benefits, it certainly has indirect benefits in that it can provide usable language input on the basis of which the student develops his or her own version of the language. Students may become competent in the new language as a consequence of instruction but not as a direct result of instruction in form. Their competency may well develop from various forms of instruction. The lack of direct benefits of instruction in language form is counterintuitive to many language teachers and students, especially those who are familiar with the large number of grammar-based language teaching programs that have produced second language users of some competence. Almost all recent studies of the relationship of experience to outcome, however, have failed to demonstrate a *direct* connection between instruction and ability.

A second major drawback to structure-based instruction is that it can mislead learners into thinking they are learning a language when, in fact, they are learning facts or information about a language. Some teachers contend that the fact that learners request or demand instruction in language structure is reason in itself to offer it. The reason is compelling, but such demands on the part of students need to be carefully examined and managed. In most cases, they are probably demanding such instruction because it is familiar and makes them feel secure, and because in learning structure the students *think* they are learning the language.

A third drawback to structural syllabi is a result of the sequencing or grading problems referred to earlier. A strictly structural syllabus prevents students from producing structures they have not been taught. Either the students have to be severely limited or controlled in their use of the new language until the needed structures have been taught, or groping and error must be tolerated or ignored until the appropriate instruction appears in the sequence. This dilemma has led to the development of "controlled communicative activities" that are intended to provide practice in using forms that have been taught.

Applications

The low transferability of structural knowledge to actual language behavior severely limits its application in language teaching settings, at least to language instruction whose goal is the ability to function in the language. If passive structural knowledge is an end in itself (i.e., explicit metalinguistic knowledge, as might be desired in a descriptive linguistics course), then extensive instruction in language structure can be useful. It is also widely held that by focusing on structure or grammar, second language accuracy is improved. But, as indicated earlier, very little evidence supports this point of view. In addition, the notion overlooks the fact that learner error involves many aspects of language besides grammar. Indeed, most local grammatical errors do not interfere with understanding or otherwise mark the person who commits them more than vocabulary or pronunciation errors. The desirable but limited role that Monitoring can play in language use can also justify a limited amount of teaching of language form.

In some settings, however, a structural definition of the language being taught may be the only one possible. This is often the case when the language is being taught in locations that are removed from the language's native-speaking communities. Given the limited goals and resources of such teaching, it may be that a small amount of structural knowledge of the language is all that the learner can expect to take away. There may even be cases in which, for political or cultural reasons, the sponsors of the instruction may not want the cultural values of the language to accompany the language instruction. In such cases, instruction limited to the structure of the language may be all that is possible.

Beyond these general remarks, space does not allow further discussion of the eternal dispute over whether grammar or structure can or should be taught to bring about second language behavior. Proponents of structural instruction still argue that structures can be taught and learned, and eventually appear as natural language behavior. Until objective evidence supports this as a general and direct rather than an exceptional or indirect route to second language ability, defining language instructional content in terms of structural information will at best detract from more useful instructional content. The primary role for the structural syllabus seems to be to instruct learners in aspects of the new language that are cognitively accessible and useful to them (the easy rules) under the limited conditions that time and the conditions of speech or writing allow.

A more complex, and more common, role for structural content is to serve as the organizing framework for other types of language instructional content, such as situations (dialogues), notions and functions, and higher-level language skills. Such an organizing function may obscure or dilute the characteristics of the structural syllabus reviewed here, but the basic functions of such content remain the same. The question of combining types of content into actual teaching syllabi will be considered in Chapter 9.

4
The Notional/Functional Syllabus

The notional/functional syllabus is the best known of contemporary language teaching syllabus types. It is, however, also the object of a great deal of misunderstanding. On the one hand, while notional/functionalism has been referred to as an "approach" (Brumfit & Johnson, 1979; Widdowson, 1979), it has never been described as anything other than a type of content of language instruction that can be taught through a variety of classroom techniques. On the other hand, notional/functionalism has been closely associated with what has been called "communicative language teaching" (Brumfit & Johnson, 1979; Richards & Rodgers, 1986; Widdowson, 1979), a rather amorphous view of language teaching that has been referred to as a method but is really a collection of different approaches and procedures clustered around notional/functional content.

Because of its broad scope, its confusion with instructional method, and its own lack of definition, notional/functionalism is difficult to describe clearly. A narrow perspective is taken here, viewing the notional/functional movement only in terms of a means for defining instructional content. In this sense, notional/functional syllabi have much in common with structural syllabi in that both are subject to a variety of interpretations and can be associated with a variety of methodologies.

Notional/functionalism grew out of a functionally oriented linguistic tradition that has long existed in Britain. Rather than examine language in isolation from its uses and social context, British linguists such as Firth (1957) and Halliday (1973) have insisted that adequate descriptions of language must include information on how and for what purposes and in what ways language is used. The philosophical work of Austin (1965) provided the basis for much of the recent analysis. In the United States, the sociolinguistic work of Hymes (1972) and others on communicative competence provided much of the theoretical basis for notional/functionalism in language teaching.

At its simplest, notional/functionalism is, in Richards and Rodgers' (1986) terms, a theory of language. It holds that basic to language are the uses to which it is put. If language is seen as a relationship between form and function, notional/functionalism takes the function side of the equation as primary and the form side as secondary. For example, rather than regarding the future tense form (with *will*) in English as basic and discussing the uses to which it can be put (e.g., talking about the future, making promises) as secondary, in a functional view of language, notions such as *future* and functions such as *promising* are considered basic and the future tense form is discussed as one way of realizing these notions and functions. Figure 4.1 presents the two different types of relationship.

Other interpretations and applications have elaborated on notional/functionalism, but the most basic point of the movement in language teaching is that categories of language use rather than categories of language form have been taken as the organizing principle for instruction.

While the categories used to talk about language form are familiar—noun, verb, statement, question, present tense, subordinate clause, and so on—the categories of language use are much less well known. Notional/functionalism defines them in two ways. First, *notions,* or categories of meaning, are what Wilkins (1976) has called semanticogrammatical categories, which are usually characterized by interaction between categories of meaning and grammatical forms in most languages. Examples of notions are *time, duration, quantity, agent, instrument, place,* and many others.

The second category of language use is *functions,* or the uses to which language forms are put, what Finocchiaro and Brumfit have called the "communicative purpose(s)" of language (1983, p. 13). Examples are *agreement, greeting, approval, prediction, requesting directions, apologizing,* and so on. An excellent listing of functional categories for teaching second or foreign languages can be found in van Ek (1976) and Finocchiaro and Brumfit (1983).

Each notion or function can be associated with a variety of forms, of course. *Instrumentality* can be expressed with prepositions (e.g., *"by* bus," *"with* an axe"), verbs (e.g., *"used* an axe," *"chopped"*), and with prepositional phrases (e.g., *"by chopping it"*). *Future time* can be expressed by future tense forms (e.g., "I'*ll* go tomorrow," "I'*m going to* go tomorrow"), present tense forms (e.g., "I *leave* tomorrow"), or present con-

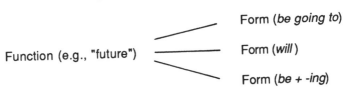

Figure 4.1. Differing relationships between form and function

tinuous forms (e.g., "I*m* leav*ing* tomorrow"). In this sense, notional/functionalism is not really new. In structural teaching, forms are primary, and indications are often (but not necessarily) made as to how the forms can be used. In notional/functionalism, the uses are primary and forms are supplied as necessary.

The determination of what notions, functions, and forms to include in a teaching syllabus is often regarded as part of notional/functionalism. Actually, notional/functionalism is a procedure for designing a syllabus or choosing content for a specific syllabus, but it is not a part of the content of the syllabus itself. Determining specific syllabus content involves examining the type of discourse the learners are going to need to engage in, noting the notions and functions and the specific forms that are used to express them in the types of discourse involved, and putting them together into a language-teaching syllabus (see Munby, 1978, for a detailed description of this type of procedure). This teaching toward specific discourse types, based on an analysis of the discourse, is one reason why notional/functionalism is often called "communicative." A second reason is simply that by teaching the association of form and meaning, communicative ability will be more likely to result than if form is taught alone. A third reason is that many applied linguists active in the notional/functional movement realized that both the content and not just the procedures of language teaching had to be expanded and modified in order to develop appropriate functional ability in students.

It is important to note, though, that notional/functionalism was initially associated with a cognitive type of learning theory that called for explicit presentation of language material, conscious recognition, and practice. More recently, it has begun to incorporate experiential learning theory, similar to Krashen's acquisition theory (Krashen, 1982), and to use techniques such as creating information gaps and problem-solving tasks as classroom activities (Richards & Rodgers, 1986).

Sequencing and grading of language material do not seem to be of major concern to notional/functional syllabus designers. Little in the literature discusses principles for sequencing material, and the question is rarely raised. Littlewood (1981) mentions only the criterion of simplicity of form for sequencing specific functions. Finocchiaro and Brumfit (1983) note that "selection and gradation is more flexible than in the past" (p. 40), and invoke the criteria of learners' need for functions, preexisting linguistic knowledge, grammatical complexity of the structures needed, and the length of utterance needed to perform some function.

Selection of material was discussed earlier. When functions associated with multiple forms are the basis for instruction, it is clear that some selection must be made. In the most general approach to notional/functional syllabus design, that of the European unit/credit system (van Ek, 1976), the determination was made as a result of individual and committee work using any means available to determine what the linguistic needs of educated adult learners in the European community would be. A general European syllabus was designed on that basis, a syllabus that would provide a basis for foreign language teaching to adults throughout Europe. Munby (1978) presents a detailed process for carrying out an analysis and turning it into a syllabus. The emerging field of discourse analysis provides much of the basis for selection of instructional content.

Notional/functional syllabi have been around for a much shorter time than structural ones, although aspects of them certainly have a longer history. Much misunderstanding and lack of definition still surround them, in addition to the confusion resulting from various connotations of the term "communicative." Problems in using them are similar to the problems that have arisen with structural syllabi—low transferability and sequencing difficulties. When combined with a cognitive theory of learning and not combined with more interactional and experiential classroom activities, notional/functional syllabi become little different from structural syllabi, a point noted by Widdowson (1979):

> The notional syllabus, it is claimed, develops students' ability to do this [become communicatively competent] by accounting for communicative competence within the actual design of the sylla-

bus itself. This is a delusion because the notional syllabus presents language as an inventory of units, of items for accumulation and storage. They are notional rather than structural isolates, but they are isolates all the same. (p. 248)

Examples
of Notional/Functional Syllabi

The major source of information on the content of notional/functional syllabi is van Ek (1976), who presents the general syllabus for the European unit/credit system, plus inventories of notions and functions and their formal exponents. A number of textbooks, many British, some American, have been written using notions and functions as their content. Two widely used series are the *In Touch* and *Life Styles* series, the former (a series for beginning students) by Castro and Kimbrough (1980) and the latter (an intermediate series) by Lozano and Sturtevant (1981). Both use a situational organization with functional content. A sample unit from each follows.

What's the matter?

Talking about sickness
Making a suggestion
Accepting or rejecting a suggestion
Making a request
Agreeing to a request

(Castro & Kimbrough, 1980)

Do you want to come with me?

Invite someone to do something
Refuse an invitation
Ask for and give information about people
Offer to do something
Accept an offer

Ask someone to give a message to another person
Mention a condition for doing something

(Lozano & Sturtevant, 1981)

Finocchiaro and Brumfit provide a sample "curriculum" (i.e., syllabus) that illustrates the organizing role of functions and the possible relationship of the functions to situations, structures, and activities (see Fig. 4.2).

Positive Characteristics of Notional/Functional Syllabi

Without doubt, including information about how language is used in a teaching syllabus potentially increases the usefulness of language instruction (Finocchiaro & Brumfit, 1983). Reductionists who teach according to a narrow definition of language (e.g., the grammatical system, much vocabulary) can often demonstrate dramatic results in the short term but still fail to develop learners' overall ability to function in a new language. The greatest strength of the notional/functional syllabus is that it includes information about language use that structural syllabi do not. If the content of an appropriate notional/functional syllabus can be learned, then the students will be better able to function in written or spoken interaction. They will have more experience with, and knowledge about, which linguistic forms do what in the new language, and they will have had exposure to at least some real or simulated interaction in the language. They may view the language less as an abstract system of elements and rules, and more as a communicative system.

At the same time, common sense says that the more specific instruction is, the more useful it will be. If notional/functional syllabi are based on accurate and adequate analyses of the types of discourse the learners will need to engage in, and if the learners continue according to their plan, then notional/functional syllabi have a higher probability of developing effective users of a new language, within a limited domain, in a relatively short time. Such success is a result of the intrinsic relationship between form and function on which notional/functional syllabi are based.

A MINI-CURRICULUM

Title and Function	Apologizing	Requesting directions	Expressing frustration
Situation	Department store (returning something)	At the bus stop	Home (dinner guests late)
Communicative Expressions or Formulas	*I'm sorry. Would it be possible ...?*	*I beg your pardon. Could you tell me ...?*	*How inconsiderate! Why couldn't they have telephoned?*
Structures	Simple past, present perfect	Interrogatives (simple present) Modal—*must*	*be + Ved* *It's* (time)
Nouns	*shirt*	names of places	*food, dessert, roast*
Verbs	*buy, wear*	*must get to, get off, take*	*ruin, spoil, serve*
Adjectives	*small*		*late*
Adverbs	*too*	*how, where*	*so*
Structure Words	*you*	*us*	
Miscellaneous	dates	numbers	time, numbers
Activities	Aural comprehension; indirect speech; changing register	Reading questions and answers; cloze procedures; dictation	Role play; aural comprehension; dicto-comp

Fig. 4.2. Syllabus with functions as organizing principle

Note. From *The Functional-Notional Approach: From Theory to Practice* by Mary Finocchiaro and Christopher Brumfit. Copyright © 1983 by Oxford University Press, Inc. Adapted by permission.

Negative Characteristics of Notional/Functional Syllabi

As suggested earlier, notional/functional syllabi that remain simple series of isolated form-function pairings will do little to develop interactional and communicative ability because these isolated functions are not synthesized into discourse. If notions and functions are taught according to cognitive learning theory, then there is no reason to believe that such instruction will be much more effective than structurally based instruction.

A converse of one of the strengths of notional/functional instruction is that because the content is tied to specifics of use, the instruction is less generalizable than structural content. For example, the future tense is the future tense, whether it is used to indicate action in the future, make a promise, or give an order. Thus, a few structures can be used to perform many functions. However, a student can learn the limited range of functions taught in a notional/functional syllabus and still have major structural gaps.

A third problem arises if notional/functional syllabi are limited to short utterances or exchanges involving the functions in question. Like structural syllabi, functional content can be presented entirely in short utterances and units of discourse. If this mistake is made, and larger structures of discourse are ignored, the students may be unable to handle the new language in longer, connected discourse.

A fourth potential weakness lies in the ease with which notional/functional syllabi can become primarily a vehicle for teaching what are called "routines" and "patterns" in second language acquisition studies. Routines are short, formulaic utterances generally used to perform some specific function, such as *No, thank you* for a polite refusal. "Patterns" are utterances with open slots into which various lexical items can be inserted (e.g., *Would you like to ___?*). Some notional/functional teaching tends to emphasize such routines and to teach them as the unanalyzed chunks they often are, rather than as the products of a grammatical system. While the role of routines and patterns in language acquisition is open to dispute (Dulay, Burt, & Krashen, 1982), one view is that if functions are taught as relatively frozen phrases they would be learned as such, and the unanalyzed routines would be used instead of productive language structures. Once again, this shortcoming can be overcome with appropriate instructional techniques.

Application

Proponents of notional/functional syllabi contend that they are applicable to almost any language teaching situation and that they are simply an improvement over structural and, to some extent, situational syllabi (see Finocchiaro & Brumfit, 1983). To the degree that notional/functional syllabi are either geared for general applications or adapted on the basis of specific discourse and needs analyses, they certainly have wide application.

In the development of specific teaching programs for specific purposes, notional/functional approaches to syllabus may be appropriately used to define the content of such courses. By allowing an examination of the specific functions occurring in various types of discourse, the notional/functional approach makes it somewhat easier to develop a syllabus with the appropriate emphasis than it would be with a structural syllabus.

But, as with structural syllabi, notional/functional syllabi present a problem of transfer. The claim has frequently been made that they will lead to more "communicative ability" (Littlewood, 1981, p. 1). As indicated earlier, however, this claim has never been empirically validated, and analysis of the content of notional/functional instruction provides little reason to accept such a claim. Because narrowly defined notional/functionalism offers no truly interactional experiences, and no guidance for developing discourse or strategic competence, its students are not any better prepared to communicate than students taught using more structural syllabi. It would seem that the difference between teaching from form to function and teaching from function to form would be minimal if all that is taught is a set of unanalyzed pieces of information about the new language that the learner has to synthesize on his or her own. The learners may still need real communicative and interactional experiences to acquire these abilities. More experience and controlled studies of notional/functional teaching will be necessary to evaluate their potential in meeting communicative goals of language teaching.

When combined with a more interactional methodology and an acquisition-based theory of language, notional/functional instructional content may lead to more functional ability. When this is a goal of the instructional program, a notional/functional syllabus might be an appropriate syllabus choice. For instructional programs whose primary goal is structural knowledge, the notional/functional syllabus is still a possible choice. As it relates forms to functions, the notional/functional syllabus may be an excellent way to impart conscious knowledge of the structure and function of a language.

5
Situational Syllabi

The situational syllabus has a long history in language teaching, but situational content has mostly been used as an adjunct to instruction that is primarily focused on language form and structure. Many "methods," from grammar-translation to Berlitz to modern integrated textbooks, have used examples of the language being learned in situations and settings. These range from short dialogues to lengthy themes with casts of characters acting and behaving in complex ways. Many collections of conversation or communication activities are organized in terms of situations.

It is important to realize that there is not just one situational syllabus, but many, differentiated by type of informational content and type of linguistic content. Alexander (1976) has distinguished three types of situational syllabus, differentiated by type of information: "limbo," concrete, and mythical. The limbo situation is one in which the specific setting of the situation is of little or no importance. Alexander gives the example of introductions at a party, where the setting of the party is largely irrelevant, and what is important is the particular language focus involved. The concrete situation is one in which the "situations are enacted against *specific* settings" (p. 98), and what is important is the setting and the language associated with it. Ordering a meal in a restaurant and going through customs are examples of concrete situations. The mythical situation is one that depends on some sort of fictional story line, frequently with a fictional cast of characters in a fictional place.

Among the different linguistic focuses that can be found in situations is the grammatical focus, with which situations are presented in such a way that particular structures or sets of structures are emphasized. It is possible to imagine a pronunciation focus that emphasizes particular pronunciation problems. Another is a lexical focus, whose emphasis is on some set of vocabulary items. Situations may emphasize functions, such as introduction or apology, or notions, such as time or color or comparison. Finally, situations may be constructed to present various types of discourse or interactional phenomena.

A related way to distinguish situational syllabi is to consider whether situations are presented to students in the form of completed discourse, or the students are expected to create or modify parts or all of it. Many situations are presented in full, and students are then asked to play out the same situation using their own language and, possibly, settings. On the other hand, situations can be presented as role plays, in which the students are expected to create, supply, or fill in much of the language that occurs in the situation.

The most familiar way of presenting a situation is as a dialogue, usually at the beginning of a lesson, although dialogues may occur anywhere in a lesson. The many ways in which dialogues can be handled in classrooms are not described here, but they include passive listening, active listening, and memorization; they can serve as models for student improvisation; and so on.

The topics, settings, and participants in situations can vary infinitely. For any use of language, a dialogue or situation can be created or selected to represent it. The content of situations can be completely created by materials writers or teachers or taken from real life.

One version of situations is role plays, in which learners act out or perform roles in defined situations. In role plays, the language may be provided, or the learners may ad lib the dialogue. A more sophisticated version of situations is DiPietro's scenarios (DiPietro, 1982). Scenarios require learners to play out roles in a

particular dramatic situation, usually a complex problem-solving setting with elements that the participants
do not anticipate. The situation is provided to the learner without dialogue or language, and the learners, usually in a group, write or prepare the language and perform the scenario. Alexander (1976) suggests that situations be personalized by putting students' names and
personalities into the situations.

With any language instructional content that attempts to incorporate some sort of language use, the
important distinction between "real" and "realistic"
(Taylor, 1982) must be kept in mind. Language that is
created for the classroom but intended to mirror actual
occasions of language use is merely "realistic" at best.
Language that actually occurs outside of the classroom,
with few artificial constraints, is "real." Most classroom dialogues are, at best, semirealistic.

Only rarely do situations make up the entire content
of a language course. Usually they are used to *present*
new material, providing examples of the phenomena
being taught, and are followed by other, more focused
exercises. Situations in the form of dialogues or role
plays may also be used to *practice* material that has
been presented in more isolated form. Situational material in many forms may be used simply to *provide
comprehensible input* (Krashen, 1982) to learners. Some
conversational courses may rely on situational material
almost exclusively.

Because of the wide variety of types and applications
of situational content, it is not associated with any
specific theory of learning. Situational content has been
used with audio-lingual (behaviorist), cognitive, and
experiential (acquisition-based) instruction. Situational
syllabi are also associated with various theories of language. A syllabus that relied almost exclusively on
realistic situations, rather than contrived or artificial
situations devised simply to exemplify linguistic structures, would, however, be most closely associated with a
broadly communicative view of language and an experiential theory of learning.

Examples of Situational Syllabi

As already indicated, situations rarely make up the entire content of a language course. They may, however, form the backbone or continuing story line of a course. One example of this is the story line that unifies the integrated course text, *Intercom*. A representative list of the situations used in the continuing story is as follows:

1. What's in the news
2. More news
3. Fun and games
4. TV news: Fire at the Ritz
5. Newspaper headlines
6. At the dentist's office
7. A weight problem
8. On a diet
9. A visit to the doctor
10. The wedding
11. Vacation places
12. Travel plans
13. On the way
14. Away from home

(Yorkey, Barrutia, Chamot, Rainey de Diaz, Gonzalez, Ney, & Woolf, 1984, Book 3, pp. iii-iv)

Another representative list of situations is taken from a supplementary conversation text:

The pet shop
The service station
Advertising
Downtown
Fire!
The working woman
The universe
Housework

(Dobson & Sedwick, 1975, p. vii)

Positive Characteristics of Situational Syllabi

Situational syllabi can lead more directly than others to learners' ability to communicate in specific settings. This aspect of situational syllabi may not necessarily be a strength. If the setting in which the language is to be used is relatively closely represented by the language in the pedagogical situation, then transfer may take place. To the degree that there is a mismatch, or that there is unpredictability in the real-life situation, then frustration and lack of transfer may be evident. When learners are being trained for highly specific and predictable settings, situations can indeed be useful.

Situations provide contexts of discourse in which form and meaning coincide. Students are not asked to learn disembodied forms with multiple potential meanings or uses, but to hear and use the forms in contexts that illustrate and reinforce the form-meaning relationship. In this way, situations can break the sentence-level barrier and demonstrate to learners, to some degree, how language operates in larger units of discourse.

The use of situations in language teaching can help to provide some social and cultural information about the language and its users in a nondidactic way. Well-prepared situations can show how native speakers act and what they talk about and are concerned about.

Negative Characteristics of Situational Syllabi

While situational syllabi can potentially increase transfer to language use in settings that are closely related to the instructional situations, too great a use of predetermined and artificial situations can lead to lack of transfer, as students are led to rely on prelearned routines and patterns of language use rather than creative and negotiated uses of language. Routines and patterns are unanalyzed chunks of language (e.g., *How have you been?*) that learners acquire without learning the structural elements and rules that make them up. The role of routines and patterns in language acquisition is controversial (Dulay, Burt, & Krashen, 1982), but it seems that overreliance on them can interfere with productive language learning. For those with very limited conversational goals, however, routines and patterns may be useful.

It is extremely difficult to create authentic language for instructional purposes. First, the actual patterns of use of native speakers in many situations are still unknown, and intuition is not a reliable guide. Many of the studies in the collection by Wolfson and Judd (1983) demonstrate this. Relying on intuition usually results in artificiality and inaccuracy. In addition, even when accurate native speaker norms are available, a special type of talent is required to write focused and natural dialogue, rarely found in published texts. A third problem with authenticity in situational content is its tendency to become outdated. The more specific and accurate the language associated with a situation, the more likely it will become inappropriate quickly.

A reliance on situational content can cause problems where the learners or the instructional setting do not want cultural values to accompany the language. For example, when the purpose of teaching English or other languages is academic, business-related, bureaucratic, or otherwise purely instrumental, the culture in which the language is being taught may have a low tolerance or acceptance level for the cultural values associated with the language. Unless the situations are written to reflect local values or the specific activities for which the language is being learned, they may reflect unwanted foreign language values.

As with other types of instructional content, situational syllabi present sequencing problems. Few criteria are available for determining the difficulty of situations and sequencing them in instructional syllabi. Sequencing can reflect some natural chain of events (buying the ticket, getting on the train, finding the seat, apologizing to a seat-mate, etc.), but it is difficult to control language that might occur in such sequences without, again, resorting to artificiality.

Applications

As indicated at the beginning of this chapter, situational syllabi rarely carry the entire content weight of an instructional program. One exception is the conversational course whose objective is limited conversational ability with specific topics. Another is instruction intended for learners with specific situations in which to use the language being learned, where the language that will occur is highly predictable (e.g., with waiters in restaurants). A third case for situational content is as a corrective tool for learners who have already received a great deal of formal instruction but who have weak functional ability in the language.

In general, however, situational content is most useful when mixed with other types of instructional content and used for the reasons mentioned earlier—to introduce new material, to practice material in realistic ways, to provide a continuous story line through some set of materials or a course, or to provide opportunities for learners to create their own discourse in defined situations.

Situational content is usable with learners of all ages, though it is especially useful for children who neither want nor are ready for formal analysis.

6
Skill-Based Syllabi

Much less is known about the skill-based, task-based, and content-based syllabi than about the types already discussed. This is especially true of the skill-based syllabus, a type that has not been previously identified as a separate kind of instructional content in the literature on language teaching. The term "skill" in language teaching has generally been used to designate one of the four modes of language: speaking, listening, reading, or writing (Chastain, 1976). Here, however, the term is used to designate a specific way of defining the content of language teaching.

A working definition of *skill* for this volume is a specific way of using language that combines structural and functional ability but exists independently of specific settings or situations. Examples are reading skills such as skimming and scanning; writing skills such as writing specific topic sentences and certain kinds of discourse (e.g., memos, research reports, work reports); speaking skills of giving instructions, delivering public talks, giving personal information for bureaucratic purposes, asking for emergency help over the telephone; and listening skills such as getting specific information over the telephone, listening to foreign radio broadcasts for news or military information, taking orders in a restaurant, and so on. Another, and more traditional, way of viewing skill-based instruction is what is called competency-based instruction. Competencies are similar to behavioral objectives in that they define what a learner is able to *do* as a result of instruction. Extensive lists of competencies have been developed for adult ESL (refugee and immigrant) programs in the United States.

Not all native speakers of a language are equally competent users of language. Also, individuals have varying competence in the different skill areas. For example, even though anyone reading this book may be considered a speaker of English, including many native speakers, not all are reading with the same degree of efficiency. Some are more "skilled" readers than others. At the same time, one person may be a particularly skilled reader but perform extremely poorly when required to carry on an emergency conversation on a mobile radio. Or someone who is an inefficient reader may be adept at getting people to buy waterbeds.

The ability to use language in specific ways (settings and registers) is partially dependent on general language ability, but partly based on experience and the need for specific skills. Language skills may, in fact, be limited to specific settings. Many waiters and waitresses in restaurants, and other workers in similar jobs, have learned only the English skills needed to carry out their work in the restaurant. They have learned a specific second-language skill. Preparing students to undertake higher education in a second language often involves teaching them specific skills such as note-taking, writing formal papers, and skimming and scanning while reading.

Such skills are somewhat independent of a more general language ability. Experience has shown that learners with limited overall ability in a second language learn to perform specific limited tasks but cannot always generalize to other applications of the skills in the language. Still, while teaching with specific occasions of use in mind is possible, the degree to which it is possible depends on the complexity and predictability of the task. Taking an order in a restaurant is a relatively predictable task. So is the assembly of a computer chip. To some degree, the same possibility holds for aspects of language use in academic settings, where well-defined forms and routines are supposed to occur. Nevertheless, increasing evidence shows that the predictability that is often assumed may be a matter of folklore, and academic language use may be as varied and unpredictable as any other.

To the degree that situations of language use and the needs of learners can be defined and matched, it is sometimes possible to teach or emphasize specific types of language use and to teach toward them. To some degree, skill-based syllabi have been used in language for specific purposes (LSP) programs, for learners who have some more or less well-defined activity they need to carry out in the second language. Actually, such programs have used a combination of structural, functional, situational, and skill-based content.

Skill- or competency-based syllabi are also becoming widely used in adult education ESL programs, especially programs for immigrants and refugees. The Mainstream English Language Training Project (MELT) (U.S. Dept. of Health & Human Services, 1985) is an excellent example of this type of syllabus. The motivation for their use in such programs seems to come from the program designers' goals of making the students as functionally competent in society and in the work place in as short a time as possible. The volume *From the Classroom to the Workplace: Teaching ESL to Adults,* published by the Center for Applied Linguistics (1983), is an excellent survey of the concerns of life skills and vocational ESL and the role of skill- and competency-based instruction.

Skill-based instructional content often reflects a reductionist theory of language, which views the overall language system as reducible, at least for teaching purposes, to specific skills or applications. At its worst, reductionism embraces the notion that specific skills can be grafted onto limited general ability (according to which a 5-year-old can learn to play virtuoso violin pieces). More generally, the reductionist view holds that language as it is used in some specific ways is formulaic and predictable.

Another approach to skill-based instruction addresses general or overall language ability *through* specific skill instruction. In this approach, instruction in specific skills is provided in addition to instruction designed to develop global language ability. The skills are presented broadly and with varied and variable applications (e.g., intensive reading of many different types of texts) so that specific skills and global ability are developed simultaneously.

Skill-based instruction is not associated with any specific theory of learning. The general theory is that the learning of complex behaviors such as language is best facilitated by breaking them down into small bits (skills), teaching the bits, and hoping that the learner will be able to put them together when actually using them. This notion is shared by many approaches to instructional content in language teaching.

Examples of Skill-Based Syllabi

One example of a skill-based syllabus is used in an advanced-level reading course for students preparing for higher education:

Guessing vocabulary from context
Scanning of nonprose material
Reading for the main idea
Using affixes as clues to meaning
Inferencing
More scanning of nonprose material
Summarizing readings
More work on affixes
Dictionary work
Restatement of informational content
More inference work
More affix work
More restatement
More inference
Analysis of paragraph structure
More affix work
Critical reading skills
Using context clues
Using expectations

(1983, pp. 477-478)

Examples of some competencies in adult education ESL are as follows:

Student will be able to identify common food items from each food group.

Student will be able to read name and price labels.

Student will be able to identify coins by name (e.g., nickel, dime) and amount.

Student will be able to give correct change.

Student will be able to identify family members by name and relationship.

Student will be able to write name, address, telephone number, and age in appropriate place on form.

(Center for Applied Linguistics, 1983, p. 17)

Positive Characteristics of Skill-Based Syllabi

Skill-based content is most useful when learners need to master specific types of language uses, either exclusively or as part of broader competency. For example, students planning to work in higher education in a second language obviously need broad proficiency in the language. It is impossible to predict all of the kinds of language and information they will encounter or need. On the other hand, it is possible to predict at least that these students will need specific reading and note-taking skills, the skill of comprehending academic lectures, and the ability to do certain types of academic writing. Graduate students who need to read limited types of second language material in specific fields need only those specific reading comprehension skills. Recently arrived immigrants and refugees need immediate abilities in the practicalities of daily life (housing, food, health, social services, law), and those being trained for work need specific skills in comprehending work instructions. These immediate needs may be subordinate to a more general proficiency in the new language. A military intelligence officer being trained to monitor enemy radio broadcasts may need no speaking or productive skills, but only certain narrowly defined listening comprehension skills using the medium of the radio and tape-recorder and dealing with the informational content of military intelligence. Thus efficiency and relevance of instruction are major strengths of the skill-based syllabus.

Relevance to student-felt needs or wants is an advantage of the skill-based syllabus because learners who know what they need to do with the language generally show great acceptance of instruction that is clearly directed toward their goals.

Negative Characteristics of Skill-Based Syllabi

As with other types of instructional content, the drawbacks to skill-based syllabi are potential rather than absolute. Under the right circumstances, the skill-based syllabus has few drawbacks. One theoretical question is the degree to which ability to perform specific tasks in a language is dependent on or independent of overall language proficiency. If the skills are limited and predictable, and can be performed with the overall competency the learner already has, then skill instruction is unarguably effective. If there is a great degree of unpredictability in the language the learner will have to process, however, a greater degree of general proficiency will be required. The question of amount of general proficiency needed thus raises the issue of the relationship between skills instruction and general proficiency. It can be argued that teaching specific skills also addresses general language proficiency. Indeed, any meaningful second language activity probably improves overall language proficiency, but the more specialized and narrowly defined the instruction, the more unlikely it is to enhance overall proficiency. Instead, instruction in specialized language skills will remain just that, an efficient way to achieve specific language use abilities.

Serious social and philosophical questions have been raised about the social values that are contained in many skill- or competency-based instructional programs (Auerbach, 1986). It is possible that skill- or competency-based instruction that is too limited in scope can program students for particular kinds of behavior (e.g., obedience in a work setting) or isolate them from achievements and ambitions that the competencies do not prepare them for (e.g., education rather than entry-level employment).

Applications

Obviously, skill-based instruction is most appropriate when learners need specific skills, and especially when these skills are well-defined and the learners have little need for global language ability. Skill- or competency-based instruction has a valuable application in life skills and vocationally oriented language programs for adult immigrants and refugees. The practical and immediate needs of these learners is a natural application for skill-based instruction. Language programs preparing students for academic work certainly have some need for skill instruction, as do vocational language programs and especially prevocational instruction whose content is intended to be applicable to a variety of similar work situations (e.g., receiving directions, measuring, counting). All of these are LSP programs.

Skill-based instruction is probably more appropriate for adults than for children, for whom an emphasis on concrete content is more appropriate. Children, however, may need a combination of skill and content work to help develop their cognitive and academic language ability along with the new language, especially if, for example, they are limited-English-proficient (LEP) students in a public school system where the language of instruction is English. Skill-based instruction is not appropriate, in large amounts, at least, for general-purpose or beginning-level language programs in which the needs of the learners are broad or yet to be defined. In such cases, focusing on narrow skill-based applications will take instructional time away from content that is more likely to address their need for overall language proficiency.

7
The Task-Based Syllabus

The task-based syllabus is relatively little-known. It is largely based on work by Krahnke (1981, 1982), Candlin and Murphy (1986), and Johnson (1982). The defining characteristic of task-based content is that it uses activities that the learners have to do for noninstructional purposes outside of the classroom as opportunities for language learning. *Tasks* are distinct from other activities to the degree that they have a noninstructional purpose and a measurable outcome. Tasks are a way of bringing the real world into the classroom.

Task-based learning is sometimes similar to situational learning, but the content of the situations is provided by the students themselves. Tasks are also not static; that is, they should involve a process of informational manipulation and development. They should also involve informational content that the language learners do not have at the beginning of the task. Another characteristic of tasks is that they require the student to apply cognitive processes of evaluation, selection, combination, modification, or supplementation (so-called "higher-order thinking skills") to a combination of new and old information. In task-based instruction, language is not taught *per se,* but is supplied as needed for the completion of the task.

An example of a task is to have the students develop

a guidebook to their school or instructional program for actual use by other students. Immigrant students might research the availability of health care in their community and develop a guide to using health care facilities. In an academic setting, students might work on a paper or report that is actually needed for a content-area class. Beginning students might tackle the process of applying for a program or job, obtaining the forms and information necessary to complete the process.

The intent of task-based learning is to use learners' real-life needs and activities as learning experiences, providing motivation through immediacy and relevancy. The focus on processing of new and old information in an interactional manner stimulates transfer. Language form is learned through language use.

Task-based learning is structurally geared toward language learning or acquisition because the tasks are part of a language learning environment or program, are chosen in part for what they will contribute to language development, and are implemented in a way that provides as much experience and feedback as possible. The language needed to carry out tasks is not provided or taught beforehand, but discovered by students and provided by teachers and other resources as the task is carried out.

Ideally, task-based instruction can constitute the entire curriculum of a language teaching program. Because it fosters language acquisition in the broadest sense by providing maximal amounts of comprehensible input (Krashen, 1982, 1985), students should acquire the same overall language proficiency as students taught through more linguistically focused instructional approaches. The one aspect of language knowledge that may not be addressed by task-based instruction, however, is explicit metalinguistic knowledge, or the ability to make descriptive or prescriptive statements about language and manipulate language as an end in itself. If such knowledge is a desired outcome of instruction, task-based learning can be combined with more traditional types of instructional activities. Units or activities focusing on structural content can easily be incorporated into the syllabus, as need or overall program objectives dictate.

The primary theory of learning underlying task-based instruction is Krashen's acquisition theory (Krashen, 1982). Acquisition theory argues that the ability to use a language is gained through exposure to and participation in using it, that experience, not training, is necessary. The theory of language most closely associated with task-based learning is communicative, representing the full spectrum of communicative competence, including linguistic, sociolinguistic, discourse, and strategic competence (Canale, 1983). Linguistic and sociolinguistic competence is acquired through comprehensible input as the student processes the information necessary to perform the task (plus whatever instruction in language form that accompanies it); discourse competence is acquired through experiencing the various discourse types called for by the tasks; and strategic competence, or the ability to use communicative strategies, is acquired through the need for understanding during the interaction required to accomplish the tasks.

Tasks can be selected according to the students' cognitive and linguistic readiness for particular tasks, their need for the particular discourse or interactional type, and availability of resources for carrying out the tasks. Sequencing of tasks should follow some of the same criteria as for selection, plus the following: shorter and simpler tasks should be undertaken before longer and more complex ones; tasks requiring known information should come before tasks calling for new information; and tasks calling for existing ability to process information should precede those requiring new types of cognitive processing (e.g., see Bloom's (1956) taxonomy). Beginning learners need short tasks that draw on information they already possess and call for more comprehension than production. Beginners should not have to perform, for example, critical or evaluative tasks if they are not ready for them. Simple recall or combination may be more appropriate. More advanced learners may be ready to handle tasks that extend over several days or weeks, call for a great deal of new or unknown information, and require complex processing such as evaluation, comparison, integration, and presentation.

Examples of Task-Based Syllabi

Published examples cannot be provided of a fully developed task-based syllabus because syllabi must be developed for each group of learners in accordance with each setting in which the instruction will occur. Following are some examples of tasks that might be used at various levels of instruction for different types of learners.

Beginning

- preparing profiles of class members for other classes or administrators or teachers
- planning and carrying out a class outing or picnic or dinner
- producing a class cookbook containing recipes from home culture
- filling out applications for drivers' licenses, social security cards, and so on

Intermediate

- preparing a handbook to the school to be used by other students
- producing an employment procedure guide—where to go, what to do, whom to talk to
- writing various types of letters—requests for information, applications, complaints
- producing newsletters for the other students in the school

Advanced

- writing term papers for other content classes
- doing a price comparison survey of food stores
- producing collections of the learners' community folklore and folkways (like the *Foxfire* series published by Arrow Books)

Positive Characteristics of Task-Based Syllabi

Task-based instruction is potentially very powerful and widely applicable. It is suitable for learners of all ages and backgrounds. It addresses the crucial problem in language teaching—the transfer problem—directly, by using active and real tasks as learning activities. Ability to perform the instructional task is equivalent to the ability to use the language, so functional ability should be a natural outcome of the instructional experience. In addition, task-based language instruction can be the vehicle for instruction in other types of content or knowledge at the same time as it addresses language acquisition.

Task-based learning can be very effective when the learners are engaged in relatively similar out-of-class activities (social or academic). It can also be valuable for learners who have a clear and immediate need to use the language for well-defined purposes. Task-based learning can be especially useful for learners who are not accustomed to more traditional types of classroom learning or who need to learn cognitive, cultural, and life skills along with the language.

Negative Characteristics of Task-Based Syllabi

The weaknesses of task-based syllabi lie not so much in the potential effectiveness of this type of instructional content but in problems of implementing the instruction. Problems can easily arise with teachers, the instructional setting, or the students. Task-based learning requires a high level of creativity and initiative on the part of the teacher. If teachers are limited to more traditional roles or do not have the time and resources to implement task-based teaching, this type of teaching may be impossible.

Second, task-based learning requires resources beyond the textbooks and related materials usually found in language classrooms. Where there are limited resources for gaining access to information via the target language, such as when the language is being taught outside the culture where it is used, task-based instruction can be difficult to implement.

Finally, because task-based learning is not what many students expect and want from a language class, they may, at least initially, resist or object to this type of instruction. In addition, task-based instruction is not teacher-centered; instead, it requires individual and group responsibility and commitment on the part of students. If students are notably lacking in these qualities, task-based instruction may indeed be difficult to implement.

Evaluation of task-based learning can be difficult. Traditional discrete-point achievement tests are often not a good measure of the language that is acquired in task learning. Overall language proficiency, however, should be as easy to measure as with any other type of instruction. While students may be making adequate improvements in their language proficiency, the global nature of task-based learning prevents it from being measurable by some of the more restricted tests. If an educational system requires students to demonstrate progress through performance on such tests, task-based instruction may have to be limited, or it may not be appropriate at all.

Applications

Task-based learning can be applied in a number of instructional settings, essentially anywhere that real-life tasks can be devised or discovered for learners. Tasks are easier to provide when the language is being taught in a setting where it is spoken, but appropriate tasks can also be found in a foreign language setting, with reliance on printed resources and invited people for information in the target language. Task-based learning can be used with learners of all ages and backgrounds, although some uniformity of interests in a class can be an asset. Since task-based learning depends heavily on the learners' receiving comprehensible input, it is especially applicable in second-language teaching settings where the learners are surrounded by resources in the target language.

Little has been published in the way of experience with, or reports on, task-based language instruction. This type of instruction holds great promise for the teaching of languages in second language settings for both adults and children. Further work will help to define its potential contribution to the overall field of language teaching.

8
The Content-Based Syllabus

Content-based language teaching has been in existence for some time, but has only recently been recognized as a viable way of teaching language as an end in itself. In concept, content-based teaching is simple: It is the teaching of content or information in the language being learned with little or no direct or explicit effort to teach the language itself separately from the content being taught. In practice, many programs using a content-based approach have also included an instructional component specifically focusing on the target language, but such specific language instruction is not regarded as the primary contributor to target language acquisition.

Recent developments in content-based teaching are closely related to the broader issue of attempts to provide effective instruction to LEP children in public schools in the United States and Canada. One solution to the problem of limited school language proficiency has been some sort of controlled immersion in the language of the school or society. "Immersion" essentially has meant that students are given content instruction in a language they may not control well or at all; that is, they simply go to school in that language. When undertaken responsibly and informedly, immersion can maximize the students' comprehension of both the target language and the content material.

The potential for the success of immersion was established by controlled research carried out in Canada (Lambert & Tucker, 1972). In this research program, students were placed in school subject classes, starting at the kindergarden level, that were taught in languages other than their first. The results of the research demonstrated that such students had learned both the content being taught and the language in which it was taught, and that cognitive development was not slowed by such an experience.

This type of evidence, and the need to educate large numbers of non-English-speaking children in the United States and Canada, gave support to bilingual education programs in both countries as a solution to the problem of educating children who do not speak the language of the educational system. The goals of bilingual education programs have been to keep non-dominant language speakers in school, to ensure that their cognitive development continues at an acceptable rate, and to give them ability in the community language that they did not have proficiency in, leading, ideally, to bilingualism.

The problems that have arisen with this concept have led to its revision, but not abandonment. One problem has to do with the concept of immersion itself. When immersion is interpreted as the placing of students with limited proficiency in the target language in a class composed primarily of native speakers without making any provision to assist their comprehension of content and their acquisition of the target language, little content learning or language acquisition takes place. But when teaching techniques are adjusted so that students comprehend the content material as it is presented in the new language, both content and language acquisition do occur. Immersion without adjustment or assistance has been labeled "submersion" (Krashen, 1985, p. 81).

The second problem with the understanding of immersion education has to do with the students' age. It is widely believed that very young children can acquire new language naturally but that older children and adults lose this capacity and need large amounts of formal training. While there is some truth to this, recent research in language acquisition has established that adults *can* acquire languages in the same manner that children do, and that, in addition, they can take better advantage of formal instruction than children can. Studies on what is called "late immersion," or immersion that starts after the age of 11 or 12, have demonstrated that older students can benefit from content-based instruction (California State Board of Education, 1984; Genesee, Polich, & Stanley, 1977). Older students may benefit more from immersion or content-based instruction if the immersion is preceded by a period of formal instruction in the language (Lapkin & Cummins, 1984; Swain, 1984).

A small body of literature exists on content-based language instruction (Chamot, 1983, 1984; Mohan, 1979). Widdowson (1978) suggested a type of content-based teaching (incorporating aspects of task-based teaching) as a means of bringing more language use into the school classroom:

> I would argue, then, that a foreign language can be associated with those areas of use which are represented by the other subjects on the school curriculum and that this not only helps to ensure the link with reality and the pupils' own experience but also provides us with the most certain means we have of teaching the language as communication, as use, rather than simply as usage. The kind of language course that I envisage is one which deals with a selection of topics taken from the other subjects: simple experiments in physics and chemistry, biological processes in plants and animals, map-drawing, descriptions of historical events and so on. . . . It is easy to see that if such a procedure were adopted, the difficulties associated with the presentation of language use in the classroom would, to a considerable degree, disappear. The presentation would essentially be the same as the methodological techniques used for introducing the topics in the subjects from which they were drawn. (p. 16)

The learning theory associated with content-based instruction is an acquisition theory that accounts for learning without explicit instruction (Krashen, 1982; Krashen & Terrell, 1983). Content-based learning seems to be most effective with younger children, but it has also been validated for older children and adults (California State Board of Education, 1984). Some evidence (Mason, 1971) suggests that even adults in higher education programs may benefit from large doses of content instruction. Some intensive academic curricula attempt to include a component of content-based instruction by having students take content courses with language instructional support. Evidence for the success of such programs is largely anecdotal, and practical and administrative problems frequently prevent them from being attempted.

In the United States, the bilingual immersion approach is being superseded in some places by a more refined approach known as the "sheltered classroom." This is an exclusively content-focused classroom for students whose proficiency in the school language is limited. Instead of direct language instruction, the students in a sheltered classroom are given content instruction while special attention is paid to their language learning needs: greater comprehensibility of the teacher's explanations, more time to complete assignments, rich language experiences throughout the curriculum, and so on. Such controlled immersion is often, but not always, supplemented by explicit formal instruction in the target language.

The theory of language assumed by content-based instruction embraces the full range of communicative competence, including a structural component (grammatical competence), sociolinguistic and discourse competence (especially in school settings and in school discourse), and strategic competence, again as it relates to academic activities. It is a use-based theory of language that sees language as arising from the settings in which it is used. Content-based learning does not clearly distinguish form and function in teaching language but makes the new language available in the contexts of its functions and meanings.

Content-based instruction has been investigated

primarily in the context of schools, using school subject content as the vehicle for language learning and the primary instructional objective. It would be equally applicable outside of school settings, especially for children, and for adults if an adequate support and monitoring mechanism is provided. Some vocational language instruction may indeed benefit from a content-based approach. Content-based instruction has a long history as an informal method, as many language learners expose themselves to immersion experiences in the process of using the language for specific purposes, improving their competence along the way.

Examples of Content-Based Syllabi

Any content-based syllabus is by definition identical to the syllabus of a content course at any level in science, social studies, or any other school subject. Extensive reading of literature or other content material in a target language can also be seen as a type of content-based learning. A content syllabus might be supplemented with traditional, form-focused, language-intensive work on, for example, vocabulary development, spelling, specific and intensive writing activities, and so on.

Positive Characteristics of Content-Based Syllabi

The strongest point in favor of content-based instruction is that it allows school students to learn subject matter and language simultaneously, avoiding the problem of having to learn the language of instruction before experiencing the instruction and, as a result of the delay, falling behind their cohorts and experiencing delayed cognitive development.

A second point in favor of content-based instruction is that the language is learned in the context of its use, eliminating the problem of transfer from instruction to use. What is learned is language use, not an inventory of items and rules that the learner must subsequently learn how to use.

A third benefit of content-based instruction is that there is an almost perfect match between what needs to be learned and what is provided. A needs analysis, formal or informal, of what learners will need to do with the language is avoided, and the problem posed by the inevitable inaccuracy of such a needs analysis is bypassed. Students learn exactly what they need to learn.

A possible fourth benefit is the motivational aspect of content-based instruction. Students who are not motivated to learn in a class focused on language itself may acquire the language more willingly when it is used to present content material that the student finds interesting.

Negative Features of Content-Based Syllabi

Content-based instruction potentially can lead to premature fossilization or overreliance on compensatory communication strategies if learners are not carefully monitored and given appropriate feedback on their language proficiency. While the causes of fossilization and marked formal inaccuracy are not clearly understood, the absence of feedback probably contributes. Formal inaccuracy can be overcome with adequate and appropriate feedback and, perhaps, some formal instruction (see Higgs & Clifford, 1982, for a discussion of a related problem in the development of second language proficiency).

Content-based instruction is often problematic with beginning or low-level adult students, although more effective ways to use it with adults will probably be developed. Children seem to be able to use a variety of linguistic and environmental cues to gain access to a new linguistic system, while adults frequently block important information out. Adults may require some amount of analytic and formal instruction, either as preparation for content-based instruction or concurrent with it, to overcome their affective resistance and to provide them with the limited formal and meta-linguistic skills they may need to refine their second language ability.

Applications

The content-based syllabus is, obviously, most applicable in primary and secondary school settings with significant numbers of students speaking a language other than the one primarily used in the educational system. It can be used in a foreign language setting if, for example, a school has determined that its students should have academic competency in a second language. The school may then choose to teach one or more content classes in the second language, starting students from an early age. Content instruction is also, of course, applicable to LEP students, whom U.S. school systems are encountering in increasing numbers. Rather than pulling the students out of content classes for ESL instruction, or delaying content instruction until some sufficient level of English ability is reached, administrators can group such students together in a sheltered, content-based classroom and provide them with the instruction necessary to develop both types of ability simultaneously (Cummins, 1981; Krashen, 1985). Even individuals or small groups of LEP students can be taught along with English-proficient students, as long as efforts are made to ensure that the subject matter they are being taught is being presented through English in a way that is comprehensible to the student. Of course, such sheltered, content-based instruction can be, and probably always should be, accompanied by some specific language (ESL) instruction.

Content-based instruction can probably be of benefit to adults in other language and content learning settings also. Immigrants, refugees, and guest workers can be taught life skills and social information in the language of the society they will be living in, getting content and language at the same time. Vocational language instruction can follow the same model, with job skills and the accompanying language abilities being taught at the same time.

Because of limitations on instructional time and resources, content-based instruction may not be appropriate where a second or foreign language is regarded as a
school subject by itself, or where knowledge of some
narrowly specified language instructional content is
mandated or expected. One exception occurs when extensive reading in the new language is assigned, possibly as an out-of-class activity. Reading of literature or
subject-matter material in the target language can be
regarded as content-based instruction. Most literature
study in the new language may be viewed as a type of
content-based instruction. In these settings, however, it
is unlikely that junior high school social studies will be
taught in French to the students who are studying
French as a foreign language. In schools with real bilingual programs, however, where English-speaking
children take content classes in, for example, Spanish,
along with the Spanish-speaking students, content-
based teaching of a foreign language is taking place.

Testing may interfere with content-based instruction if students' achievement and progress in the educational system is measured by tests that focus on narrowly defined formal features of the target language (e.g.,
spelling, phonics, grammatical accuracy). In general,
students with global language abilities will do well on
such tests of specific knowledge even though the specifics may not have been the focus of instruction.
However, specific formal knowledge may take longer to
develop. If such tests play an important role in the educational system, content-based instruction may have to
be supplemented with some type of formal instruction.

Content-based instruction does not guarantee successful communicative ability, especially productive
ability (Mohan, 1979), unless extensive productive activities are included as part of the overall instructional
experience.

9
Choosing and Integrating Syllabi

The term *syllabus,* as used here, does not refer to a document guiding the teaching of a specific language course, but to a more theoretical notion of the *types* of content involved in language teaching and the bases for the organization of language courses.

This chapter concerns the factors affecting the choice of content to be included in a second language teaching syllabus, including the program, the teacher, and the students. Following this, several design issues relating to syllabus choice are discussed. Finally, a procedure for actually producing a syllabus for a course is outlined. This outline is brief because the question has been treated in great detail elsewhere (Dubin & Olshtain, 1986; Steiner, 1975; Yalden, 1983).

In the preceding chapters, six types of syllabus content were defined and described as ideal or isolated types. In actual teaching settings, of course, it is rare for one type of syllabus or content to be used exclusively of other types. Syllabus or content types are usually combined in more or less integrated ways, with one type as the organizing basis around which the others are arranged and related. For example, many foreign language courses are organized around a structural syllabus, with each unit or chapter focusing on several grammatical features. Accompanying the grammatical focus and organization, however, are other types of content, usually situational (dialogues) and functional (how to introduce yourself).

Basic syllabus design involves several questions. The first question concerns the types of content to include or exclude. The second is whether to combine various types of syllabus content or to rely on a single type. The third, assuming that more than one type of content will be included, is whether to use one type as basic and to organize others around it, or to sequence each type more or less independently of the other. In discussing syllabus choice and design, then, it should be kept in mind that the issue is not which type to choose but which types, and how to relate them to each other. Before this issue is discussed, three factors that affect the choice of syllabus or content in language teaching—program, teacher, and students—are examined.

Program Factors Affecting Syllabus Choice and Design

Goals and Objectives

The major determinant in choosing a syllabus type for second language teaching must be the goals and objectives of the overall instructional program; that is, the type of knowledge or behavior desired as an outcome of the instruction. This truism has not been consistently recognized. For example, for a number of years it has been widely accepted that ability to function communicatively in a second language is a desirable outcome (among others) of foreign language instruction in secondary schools and at the college level. The emphasis in much of this instruction, however, has remained on the structural and formal aspects of language, presumably under the assumption that one kind of knowledge (structural) will lead to the other (ability to function). Yet ample evidence has shown that more direct routes to functional ability are possible, using a variety of types of instructional content, such as situational, skill, and notional/functional content. Thus the relationship of the goals of instruction to the content of instruction has not always been direct.

While it may seem like an oversimplification, a useful guiding principle in second language learning is that learners learn to do what they do while they are being instructed. Students who spend their instructional time hearing, repeating, and role-playing the language of various situations will learn how to speak in those situations, but not others. Students who spend their instructional time learning social studies through the second language (content-based instruction) will learn how to use the second language in the ways that are needed to learn in similar academic content areas.

Given this general guideline, the question of the relationship of overall program goals and instructional content is one of choosing a type or types of instructional content that most closely match the goals of the program. For almost all instructional programs, it is clear that some combination of types of instructional content will be needed to address the complex goals of the program. Previous chapters identified how each type of syllabus relates to various goals and objectives. Here it is sufficient to note that for most general foreign language teaching applications, whose goal is functional ability in broadly defined settings and structural knowledge and communicative ability in specific situations, a combination of functional, structural, situational, and skill-based instruction is the probable choice. On the other hand, in some second language teaching settings, skills and tasks can be more narrowly specified, instructional resources are richer, or specific structural or formal knowledge is not required by the program for the students to succeed, and a combination of task-based, skill-based, situational, functional, and content instruction may be chosen. The specific proportions of each type have to be further determined on the basis of narrower specifications of students' need and on the basis of empirical and theoretical arguments for the need and usefulness of each type of instruction. The outcomes of each type of instructional content have been identified in the preceding chapters.

Instructional Resources

Clearly, one factor that will affect the type of syllabus or syllabi that can be chosen is the instructional resources available. Resources may include elements such as time, textbooks and other materials, visuals (films, slides, pictures), realia, and out-of-classroom resources such as other speakers of the language, radio and television programs, films, field trips, and so on.

Of these resources, textbooks certainly play the greatest role in the determination of syllabus. For many programs, they are the only determinant. Frequently, programs adopt textbooks for courses and expect teachers to use them as the sole or major source of classroom instruction. If a text already exists for a course, it is usually the basis for the course's syllabus. If a text is to be adopted, prospective texts should be examined for their adequacy as a basis for a syllabus. Space does not permit a taxonomy of available textbooks, but most major educational publishers offer textbook series for the commonly taught languages. In general, these series tend to be structurally focused and organized but include some situational and skill content. Many recent texts, especially for English language teaching, emphasize functional content and organization. No task-based texts are yet available, and content-based teaching will usually use text material intended for native speakers of the language.

The availability of nontext or supplementary text resources clearly affects the ease with which instructional content beyond the textbook can be included in a language course. For example, skill-based instruction focusing on the comprehension of native-like speech, either in conversational or in academic lecture settings, is difficult to undertake where few other speakers of the target language are available for conversation or lectures or where taped material or the means to use it is limited. Similarly, a situational lesson requiring students to ask directions to get around a town would be difficult to implement without maps, diagrams, or pictures of the town. Tasks also may require resources such as schedules, forms, reference books or other material, people, information sources, and so on.

In general, however, the resourceful instructor or instructional planner can devise resources and modify activities so that available resources can be used. An ESL textbook (Plaister, 1976), for example, makes native-like lecture and reading material available for skill instruction in academic course work almost entirely through the textbook alone, in the hands of a competent instructor. Tasks can be devised using classroom resources, such as duplicated forms to be filled out or a variety of newspaper stories about a single topic to be combined into a single, usable version by the students.

Content-based second language instruction requires the resources that are normally needed to teach the content in the native-speaker classroom, plus whatever instructional aids can help make the content more accessible and comprehensible for students with limited language ability (the sheltered classroom).

Accountability and Measurement

A final program factor affecting the choice of instructional content may be the need to make the instruction accountable to authorities or measurable by external measures—usually tests. The influence of tests on the content of instruction is a well-known phenomenon. Teachers and instructional programs often teach toward a particular kind of knowledge if it is going to be tested, even though the knowledge may not be what the students really need. One clear example has been the emphasis on teaching toward the kind of language abilities tested by the Test of English as a Foreign Language (TOEFL) in academic-preparation ESL programs in the United States. Because, until recently, the TOEFL did not test writing directly, but did include many items that seemed to require grammatical judgments, academic-preparation ESL programs have tended to stress grammar instruction and deemphasize instruction in writing. A more recent example is the impact that the new ACTFL Proficiency Guidelines seem to be having on the curricula and syllabi of foreign language teaching programs in the United States. By including evaluative criteria, for example, for understanding the spoken language as it is used on the telephone and through other electronic media, the guidelines are leading instructional programs to include more skill-based instruction with such types of language use in mind.

Teacher Factors Affecting Syllabus Choice and Design

Along with the more general program factors, teachers play a role in determining what the content of language instruction will be. A truism of teaching is that teachers tend to teach what they know. A teacher who is not familiar with the formal aspects of a language will not be likely to try to teach a grammar lesson, but might, for example, focus on the social uses (functions) of language or how it is used in various situations. On the other hand, the science teacher with one student who does not speak the language of the classroom may go ahead and teach science in the best way possible (content instruction) rather than try to give the student a special language lesson.

Some research in teacher practice suggests that language teachers do not accurately describe their own practice (Long & Sato, 1983), have contradictory and inconsistent beliefs about language teaching (Krahnke & Knowles, 1984) and tend to repeat their own experiences as students when they become teachers. As a result, teachers can have a powerful influence on the actual syllabus of a classroom even if the official or overt syllabus of the program is entirely different.

The teacher's belief system or orientation is also a major determinant of syllabus or content. A teacher may be fully knowledgeable about the linguistic structure of the language being taught but may believe that languages are best learned through experience rather than through analysis and synthesis. This teacher may then try to include as much task- and content-based instruction as possible in the class, even when the overt class syllabus might be a structural one. The teacher's ability is another potential major determinant of actual instructional content. Just as a teacher who is not knowledgeable about the formal aspects of the language cannot teach them even if the syllabus calls for it, a teacher with limited ability to use the language functionally will not be able to assist and encourage students to carry out task-based instruction. And the teacher who does not know enough about a scientific topic to discourse on it in the target language will not be able to provide content-based instruction.

Of course, teachers can be trained, but training is costly and time-consuming, and some of the research cited earlier suggests that such training is of limited benefit. The conservative position on the relationship between a teacher's beliefs and abilities and the choice of instructional content is to expect that teachers be relatively willing and able to undertake the type of instruction chosen *before* they undertake it; otherwise they will use content with which they are more comfortable at best and, at worst, flounder.

Student Factors Affecting Syllabus Choice and Design

Facts about students also affect what instructional content can be used in an instructional program. The major concerns here are the goals of the students, their experience, expectations, and prior knowledge, their social and personality types, and the number of students in a given class.

Ideally, the goals the students themselves have for language study will match the goals of the program. When this is so, the question of goals is easy to settle. Sometimes, however, programs and students have different goals. For example, one instructional program was designed to teach the English of the broadcasting profession at a vocational school. The program administrators assumed that the students' language learning goals were tied to the professional training they were receiving. Many students, however, were more interested in attaining general English proficiency to prepare them for even better positions than they were being trained for. One way to meet both sets of goals would be to increase the amount of general functional, situational, and skill content provided along with the specialized skill and structural content that was being taught.

The experience, expectations, and knowledge that students bring to the instruction can also affect syllabus choice, although the literature is curiously quiet about this factor. Many syllabus and methodological recommendations are made as though students can and will easily accept any instructional content. With children such a policy may be safer than with adults. Adults often have distinct ideas of what language instruction should be, even though these ideas may, from a professionally informed perspective, conflict with their language learning goals.

Generally, the difference between students' expectations and the instruction they receive is between instruction that focuses on form (structural content) and instruction that focuses on function (functional, situational, skill-based, or other content). Students who expect one and get the other may resist. If so, the instructor has three choices: to continue and possibly "lose" students; to "give in" to the students either completely or by compromising; or to continue with the original instructional plan while trying to convince the students over time that the program decision is appropriate. Too often, one of the first two routes is chosen, with not enough effort given to bringing the students around. For example, one group of students initially resisted engaging in task-based learning experiences, preferring the intellectual anonymity of more traditional instruction. Many strong resisters have been won over in time, however, by teachers who believed in their approach and persisted with it.

There are extremes, however, and it would be idealistic to believe that all students can be easily made to accept a type of teaching with which they are unfamiliar or uncomfortable. Some syllabus decisions may have to be made only because the students have a strong allegiance or resistance to one or another type of instruction. Two possible solutions should be kept in mind. One is that students, as described earlier, can be brought around to accepting a kind of instruction they may not initially accept.

The other technique that may be used if students are

resisting a type of instructional content that appears to be what they need (e.g., functional) in favor of one with which they are more comfortable (e.g., structural), is the *covert syllabus*. A covert syllabus simply provides a significant amount of the type of instruction thought to be appropriate for the students without calling attention to it in the course descriptions or materials. The overt syllabus may be structural, and teaching points and course organization may be stated in structural terms. However, the course might actually stress functional content, from the specific functions of various structures (notional/functional) to actual skill-, task-, or content-based instruction. The latter types might be presented to the students as "practice."

Language instruction has foundered or failed when resisted by students. Students' readiness for one or another type of instruction is, therefore, a crucial factor in deciding what syllabus type to adopt for a given teaching setting, among other decisions. Teachers and course designers must remember, however, that they are in control of the instruction and can best determine instructional needs.

Other Issues

A host of other issues affect syllabus choice in language teaching, of which a few are touched on here.

Needs Analyses

Much discussion has appeared in the literature on syllabus design in recent years about performing a needs analysis before designing a syllabus (Munby, 1978; Yalden, 1983). In concept, needs analyses are simple: the linguistic and communicative material that students will need is determined, and the teaching syllabus is developed accordingly. Unfortunately, needs analyses are difficult to perform for several reasons.

The first reason is economic. Many teaching programs simply do not have the time, financial resources, and expertise needed to carry out a really useful needs analysis. A good needs analysis requires the skills of a trained linguist as well as other professionals.

Second, needs analyses are often not practically feasible. Such analyses may require an extensive time investment. Carrying out needs analyses even on familiar activities such as doing academic work in second languages may require months of observing lectures, interviewing teachers and students, collecting examples of written work, analyzing texts, and so on. Converting the systematic analysis into a syllabus may take an equal amount of time and effort.

Finally, a needs analysis may reveal that students' needs are so broad that a useful selection of content is difficult to make. The eventual foreign language needs of high school and university students in the United States is, possibly, one example of this.

For these and other reasons, few needs analyses are ever undertaken in practice. Most often the processes of needs analysis and syllabus design occur simultaneously, with no formal needs analysis. Also, few follow-up studies are done to determine whether what is taught is actually what students most need (see Christison & Krahnke, 1986, for one such study).

The impracticality of needs analyses in relation to syllabus design is a reality that can best be handled by adding caution and skepticism to the matter of syllabus choice and design. Recognizing that decisions about instructional content may well turn out to be deficient or inappropriate, designers of instruction can choose the broadest type of content possible to ensure that the future second language needs of the students will probably be met.

Reductionism

One answer to the problems of syllabus design and learnability, as well as accountability and measurement, has been to adopt a reductionist approach to instructional content. A reductionist approach attempts to define the least that should be taught to meet some real or imagined need. In audio-lingual language teaching, for example, the amount of vocabulary students were required to learn was kept as small as possible in order to maximize learning of the structure of the target language. This reduced view of language (structure with little semantics) led to dramatic initial increases in the learning of specific structures, but seems to have contributed little to overall language acquisition.

In the teaching of ESL writing in academic settings, one approach has been to focus on teaching students the organizational patterns assumed to predominate in academic writing. Sometimes this instruction offers an idealized procedure for producing such products (a product approach). This reductionist approach to second language writing leads to a rigid and limited view of what writing is and how it is achieved, and potentially leaves students unprepared for the creative and unpredictable writing tasks they must face in real academic work.

Reductionism in syllabus design is a temptation because of the apparent success with which limited amounts of language can be taught and learned. A sometimes frustratingly slow and complex process is seemingly made simpler by eliminating many difficult aspects. Considering what students eventually need in order to succeed with a second language, however, reductionist approaches to syllabus design do more harm than good. Once again, the most practical alternative to reductionist syllabi is instructional content that provides learners with the broadest possible range of abilities and knowledge.

Flexibility of Syllabus Design

Little is mentioned in the literature about the question of how loosely or narrowly to define a language teaching syllabus. As with other aspects of syllabus design, no simple answer can be given. A narrowly defined syllabus allows little room for modification by teacher or students: They do what the syllabus predetermines for the classroom. Narrowly defined syllabi are sometimes called "teacherproof." In contrast, a loosely defined syllabus allows for more flexibility, modification, and innovation on the part of the teachers and students. The teacher's ability and resourcefulness interact with the type of syllabus to produce varying degrees of definition.

In instructional settings where teachers have insufficient time, competence in the language, instructional ability, or creativity to go beyond an assigned syllabus with set materials, a narrowly defined syllabus is preferable. Such a syllabus might also be desirable when teachers are not well trained in the type of teaching defined by the syllabus, or disagree with it. On the other hand, teachers who are well-trained, competent, resourceful, and favor the type of teaching defined might need a much less narrowly defined syllabus, and feel professionally restrained by one that is too narrowly defined.

The type of syllabus also affects the degree of definition. Any type of syllabus can potentially be narrowly defined, but structural, functional, and situational types are obviously more amenable to narrow definition than skill-, task-, and content-based syllabi. The latter types can often be defined in a general way, but many specifics, especially language specifics, may be unpredictable and have to be dealt with spontaneously. For example, while teaching business letter-writing skills, a teacher may discover that students have poor spelling or punctuation. Instruction in these more specific skills may be necessary before the overall objectives can be met. In general, structural, functional, and situational syllabi can be carefully defined so that very few unpredicted learning needs arise.

Cyclical versus Linear Syllabi

Much has been made in recent years (Dubin & Olshtain, 1986; Yalden, 1983) of a cyclical or spiraled approach to the form of a syllabus rather than a linear one. In a linear syllabus, material is dealt with once, presumably mastered by the students, and never directly taken up again. This is the concept of mastery learning, by which a series of small, discrete steps is taught and learned, and all add up to the overall behavior desired. Although many language teaching syllabi follow a linear format, the concept has been questioned for some time. Corder (1973) notes that "Language learning is not just cumulative, it is an integrative process" (p. 297), and argues for a cyclical pattern that allows language material to be dealt with repeatedly as the syllabus progresses, usually with a greater degree of complexity each time it is encountered. The cyclical design is also in harmony with current knowledge about the development of linguistic competence, as characterized by recent work in first language acquisition (Dulay, Burt, & Krashen, 1982; Ellis, 1986). Language regularities do not emerge fully and perfectly formed as a result of an instructional or other experience, but instead form gradually and with an increasing degree of refinement. A cyclical syllabus, at least in its more general features, resembles this process.

The literature shows a general preference for cyclical syllabus designs, but practical problems persist. Designing a syllabus that is both narrowly defined and cyclical may be a formidable challenge. The ordering of items is a basic theoretical issue even for a linear syllabus. Creating a cyclical one in which items were not only well sequenced relative to each other, but were also appropriately *re*sequenced in increasingly complex forms would require great amounts of intuition, guesswork, and artful juxtaposition. Nevertheless, even loosely spiraled syllabi are the preferred design for modern language teaching.

Linearity and syllabus type also interact somewhat naturally. The more narrowly that *language* material is specified, the greater the sequencing problem. But if language material is embedded in other types of instruction (i.e., situations, content, tasks), it is naturally cycled and can be dealt with as needs for it arise in the context of the larger instructional objectives. For example, in a linear structural syllabus, a place must be determined for a particular verb tense form, and most of what is deemed relevant to the knowledge and use of that form must be presented at a few specified points in the syllabus. In a cyclical syllabus, the same information reappears at several points. In a situational or other loosely defined syllabus, the verb tense form will naturally recur (with, possibly, some deliberate intervention provided by the materials or imposed by the teacher), and will recur in a variety of collocations and contexts.

Combining and Integrating Syllabus Types

Throughout this monograph, syllabus *types* have been discussed more or less ideally and independently, treating each as if it were the sole type being used in instruction. In practice, however, few instructional programs rely on only one type but combine types in various ways.

A distinction exists between combination and integration, although it is not absolute. *Combination* is the inclusion of more than one type of syllabus with little attempt to relate the content types to each other. For example, a lesson on the function of disagreeing (functional) could be followed by one on listening for topic shifts (skill) in which the function of disagreeing has no significant occurrence. Such combination frequently occurs in language teaching when various communicative or "fluency" activities (i.e., skills, tasks) are added on to a structural, functional, or situational syllabus. Little or no attempt is made to relate the content of the two types of instruction.

Integration is when some attempt is made to interrelate content items. For example, if, after a structural lesson on the subjunctive, students were asked to prepare stories on the theme, "What I would do if I were rich," the two types of instruction would be integrated.

Integration is obviously more difficult and complex to undertake than combination. Integration may seem to be the preferred way to use different syllabus or content types, and in some ways this perception is accurate. Instruction that reinforces and relates various syllabus and content types is probably more effective than instruction that is divided into discrete compartments. On the other hand, again, when specific knowledge and behavioral outcomes are desired, discrete combinations may be preferable to fully integrated syllabi. For example, if it is true that instruction in form is directly usable by learners mostly for Monitoring (Krashen,

1982), then it may be that structural or formal syllabi should make up, as Krashen suggests, a limited but separate part of the overall curriculum, with the objective of enabling students to use the structural knowledge in test-taking and editing settings, and not of enabling them to gain active control over the use of the structures in discourse.

Another argument in favor of combination stems from the finding that much of early second language behavior is a combination of formulaic language use (use of memorized chunks of language for particular functions) and more creative and synthesized applications of rules (Ellis, 1986). It may be that some situational or functional content can be included with the objective of providing the learners with the formulas and routines they need for immediate and specific communication, and other types of instruction can be used to foster their overall language acquisition.

Once again, a practical answer to the problem of integration and combination resides in the choice of syllabus itself. If syllabus types on the lower end of the scale predominate in a program (i.e., structural, functional, situational), then the problem of integration is more acute. Syllabus types on the higher end of the scale integrate language material naturally, or at least provide natural contexts for integration, because they contain more complex discourse, and language material, skills, and informational content occur in meaningful ways and in larger contexts. Imagine, for example, an instructional *task* that requires students to draw information about a tourist attraction from reading and interviews to analyze, evaluate, and synthesize into a guide to the attraction. They will encounter a number of language forms and functions, and any difficulty will be addressed by the instruction. In addition, of course, unintegrated instruction in various structural or skill matters might also be included.

For both practical and theoretical reasons, then, integration of syllabus types may not always be preferred over simple combination. If other criteria call for a reliance on structural, situational, or functional content, then integration is a higher priority. If more analytic syllabus types are used, however, the problem of integration may not be as complex and may be handled better through natural integration of content.

Before leaving the matter of combination and integration of syllabus types, it would be useful to examine two recent recommendations for a combination approach to syllabus design. Yalden (1983) proposes the Proportional approach. After distinguishing, to some degree, structural and other types of instructional content, she recommends a relatively unintegrated approach in which structural content is provided in increasingly smaller proportions relative to instruction based on increasingly larger units of discourse as overall language proficiency increases. The structural material, it is assumed, provides formal resources for the learner in the acquisition of more complex language functions and skills and in carrying out more complex communicative tasks.

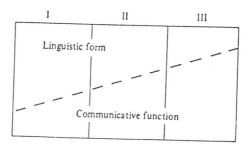

Figure 9.1. Three levels in a balanced system.

Note. From *The Communicative Syllabus: Evolution, Design, and Implementation* (p. 122) by J. Yalden, 1983, Oxford, England: Pergamon. Copyright 1983 by Pergamon. Reprinted by permission.

Krashen (1985) takes a stronger position on the limitations of structural content and describes general curriculum types for six types of teaching programs: university ESL programs (English for academic purposes), foreign language teaching in high schools and universities, programs for limited-English-proficient students in U.S. public schools, foreign language programs in elementary schools, adult education programs, and special-purpose language teaching programs. Like Yalden, Krashen does not make the same distinctions in content that are made here, but he does distinguish structural and other formal instruction from content with more complex discourse, especially content-based instruction. Figure 9.2 illustrates Krashen's recommendations for high school and university foreign language teaching. In the figure, "Natural Approach" refers to learning that is mostly situational, skill-based, task-based, and content-based. "Grammar study for Monitor use" refers to instruction focusing on structural content.

I   General language teaching
    A Natural Approach: focus on topics of general interest
    B Grammar study for Monitor use

II Sheltered subject-matter teaching
    A Short courses on geography, current events, history of speakers of the target language
    B Elective pleasure reading
    C Grammar study
       1. continued study for Monitor use
       2. as subject matter (linguistics)

III Partial mainstream: works of single author or groups of authors in familiar settings

IV Full mainstream: the survey course

Figure 9.2. High school and university foreign language curriculum.

Note. From *The Input Hypothesis: Issues and Implications* (p. 78) by S. Krashen, 1985, New York: Longman. Copyright 1985 by Longman. Reprinted by permission.

The two examples serve to illustrate the principle of combination or integration of syllabus types embodied in recent recommendations for syllabus design. Both examples recognize the different outcomes and objectives of different types of content and provide a place for a range of types of instruction in the overall curriculum.

In summary, then, a simple principle emerges from the question of syllabus choice and integration: Always choose the syllabus type that includes the broadest and most comprehensive representation of language functions and discourse types and skill-, task-, or content-based learning. In this way the syllabus designer ensures that two general goals of language instruction will be addressed. First, the bridge to communicative ability will be easier to cross because the problem of synthesis of knowledge and transfer of training is minimized. Secondly, the objectives the students are required to meet will not be so narrow as to handicap them when they are faced with actual occasions of language use. In applying this principle, it is clear that skill-, task-, or content-focused second language instruction may often have to be supplemented with instruction in more specific aspects of the language.

A Practical Guide
to Syllabus Choice and Design

The resources available for actual language teaching syllabi have been described in this monograph, along with some of the constraints on choosing and combining them. By now it is clear that no single type of content is appropriate for all teaching settings, and the needs and conditions of each setting are so idiosyncratic that specific recommendations for combination are not possible. In addition, the *process* of designing and implementing an actual syllabus warrants a separate volume. Several books are available that address the process of syllabus design and implementation both practically and theoretically. Steiner (1975) does not really address the question of different syllabus types, and is concerned primarily with the process of defining behavioral objectives for language courses. Nevertheless, she does deal at some length with the practical problems of relating syllabus construction to matters of textbooks, teachers' abilities and orientations, course goals and objectives, and various behavioral outcomes. Focused on teaching foreign languages in public school settings in the United States, her book is a valuable source of practical guidance in making syllabus choices.

More recently, Dubin and Olshtain (1986) have reviewed the problem of course design, including curriculum and specific syllabus questions, for ESL and EFL settings. Once again, without making specific recommendations, they describe much of the process of course design, from setting goals and objectives, through needs analysis and resource evaluation, to syllabus preparation and materials preparation. The authors consider at length many of the practical and theoretical constraints on syllabus design that were briefly reviewed here.

These books, among others (see the Annotated Bibliography, p. 93), can help language course designers make specific decisions for their own programs. However, a set of guidelines for the process is provided next.

Ten steps in preparing a practical language teaching syllabus:

1. Determine, to the extent possible, what outcomes are desired for the students in the instructional program. That is, as exactly and realistically as possible, define what the students should be able to do as a result of the instruction.

2. Rank the syllabus types presented here as to their likelihood of leading to the outcomes desired. Several rankings may be necessary if outcomes are complex.

3. Evaluate available resources in expertise (for teaching, needs analysis, materials choice and production, etc.), in materials, and in training for teachers.

4. Rank the syllabi relative to available resources. That is, determine what syllabus types would be the easiest to implement given available resources.

5. Compare the lists made under Nos. 2 and 4. Making as few adjustments to the earlier list as possible, produce a new ranking based on the resources constraints.

6. Repeat the process, taking into account the constraints contributed by teacher and student factors described earlier.

7. Determine a final ranking, taking into account all the information produced by the earlier steps.

8. Designate one or two syllabus types as dominant

and one or two as secondary.

9. Review the question of combination or integration of syllabus type and determine how combination will be achieved and in what proportion.

10. Translate decisions into actual teaching units.

This guide is intended as a general procedure to follow in making syllabus decisions for specific instructional programs. It is expected that quite different designs will emerge for each application, and this is as it should be. What is important in making *practical* decisions about syllabus design is that all possible factors that might affect the teachability of the syllabus be taken into account. This can be done only at the program level. By starting with the definitions of syllabus type described in this monograph and tailoring the choice and integration of the types according to local needs, a principled and yet practical solution to the problem of appropriateness and effectiveness in syllabus design can be reached.

Annotated Bibliography
of Basic Works
on Syllabus Design

1. **Alexander, L.G.** (1976). Where do we go from here? A reconsideration of some basic assumptions affecting course design. *English Language Teaching, 30*(2), 89-103.

   Makes some excellent suggestions for implementing functional syllabi, but is primarily a thorough review of situational syllabi with a typology of situational syllabi and recommendations for using them.

2. **Corder, S.P.** (1973). *Introducing applied linguistics* (Chap. 12). Harmondsworth: Penguin.

   Older, predating notional/functional syllabi. Clear and useful review of structural content of syllabi and sequencing of structural content. Also touches on situational syllabi.

3. **Dubin, F., & Olshtain, E.** (1986). *Course design: Developing programs and materials for language learning.* Cambridge: Cambridge University Press.

   Not specifically on syllabus design, but reviews the process of developing course goals and objectives and relating them to syllabus content and instructional materials. Communicatively oriented, but not in a narrowly notional/functional sense. Useful and practical.

4. **Johnson, K.** (1982). *Communicative syllabus design and methodology.* Oxford: Pergamon Press.

   A collection of papers discussing the role of various types of "semantic" or notional/functional syllabi from a theoretical and "exploratory" perspective. The relationship between notional/functional syllabi, task-based instruction, and communicative teaching methodologies is also considered. The author recommends a "multidimensional" approach to syllabus design, integrating notional/functional material with other types. He also suggests methodological solutions to some problems of syllabus design.

5. **McKay, S.** (1980). Towards an integrated syllabus. In K. Croft (Ed.), *Readings in English as a second language* (pp. 72-84). Boston: Little-Brown.

   Reviews structural, functional, and situational syllabi. Recommends combination, with functional predominating. Thorough review of issues.

6. **Mohan, B.** (1979). Relating language teaching and content teaching. *TESOL Quarterly, 13* (2), 171-182.

   Discussion of the relation between language and content teaching. Presents various models of the relationship and recommends a closer connection.

7. **Mohan, B.** (1977). Toward a situational curriculum. *On TESOL '77.* Washington, DC: Teachers of English to Speakers of Other Languages.

   Breaks situations into four types so situational syllabi can be more easily organized and related to other aspects of language and teaching.

8. **Munby, J.** (1978). *Communicative syllabus design.* Cambridge: Cambridge University Press.

Major theoretical work in specific-purpose syllabi. Rigorous and exhaustive. Difficult to apply.

9. **Shaw, A.M.** (1977). Foreign language syllabus development: Some recent approaches. *Language Teaching and Linguistics: Abstracts, 10*(4), 217-233.

Basic review of syllabus design, including grammatical, situational, topical, notional, and "opera-
tional." Focuses on communicative syllabi. Useful
discussion of the process of syllabus design.

10. **Steiner, F.** (1975). *Performing with objectives*. Rowley, MA: Newbury House.

An older work more concerned with setting behavioral objectives for high school foreign language
study than with syllabus design *per se*. It is, however, valuable in its discussion of the process of
developing curricula and syllabi and relating them
to the realistic and practical concerns of teachers,
administrators, and existing texts.

11. **Stratton, F.** (1977). Putting the communicative syllabus in its place. *TESOL Quarterly, 11*(2), 131-141.

Discusses limitations on and recommendations
for notional/functional syllabus design. Recommends a combination of structural and functional
syllabi.

12. **van Ek, J.A.** (1976). *The threshold level for modern
language learning in schools*. London: Longman.

Basic reference work on notional/functional syllabi. Contains definition of basic concepts and extensive lists of notions, functions, and exponents.

13. **Wilkins, D.A.** (1976). *Notional syllabuses*. Oxford:
Oxford University Press.

Discusses structural, situational, and notional
approaches to syllabus design. Provides historical
and theoretical perspectives. Good section on design
and implementation of communicative syllabi.

References

Alexander, L.G. (1976). (1976). Where do we go from here? A reconsideration of some basic assumptions affecting course design. *English Language Teaching, 30*(2), 89-103.

Allwright, R. (1979). Language learning through communicative practice. In C.J. Brumfit & K. Johnson (Eds.), *The communicative approach to language teaching*. Oxford: Oxford University Press.

Auerbach, E.R. (1986). Competency-based ESL: One step forward or two steps back? *TESOL Quarterly, 20*(3), 411-429.

Austin, J.L. (1965). *How to do things with words*. Cambridge, MA: Harvard University Press.

Azar, B. (1981). *Understanding and using English grammar*. Englewood Cliffs, NJ: Prentice-Hall.

Birckbichler, D., & Omaggio, A. (1978). Diagnosing and responding to individual learner needs. *Modern Language Journal, 52*(7), 336-345.

Bloom, B.S. (Ed.) (1956). *A taxonomy of educational objectives* (Handbook 1). *Cognitive domain*. New York: McKay.

Brown, H.D. (1980). *Principles of language learning and teaching*. Englewood Cliffs, NJ: Prentice-Hall.

Brumfit, C.J., & Johnson, K. (Eds.). (1979). *The communicative approach to language teaching.* Oxford: Oxford University Press.

California State Board of Education. (1984). *Studies in immersion education.* Sacramento, CA: Office of Bilingual Bicultural Education, California State Board of Education.

Canale, M., & Swain, M. (1980). Theoretical bases of communicative approaches to second-language teaching and testing. *Applied Linguistics, 1,* 1-47.

Candlin, C., & Murphy, D. (Eds.) (1986). *Language learning tasks* (Vol. 7, Lancaster Practical Papers). London: Pergamon.

Carroll, J.B. (1966). The contributions of psychological theory and educational research to the teaching of foreign languages. In A. Valdman (Ed.), *Trends in language teaching.* New York: McGraw-Hill.

Castro, O., & Kimbrough, V. (1980). *In touch.* New York: Longman.

Chamot, A. (1983). Toward a functional ESL curriculum in the elementary school. *TESOL Quarterly, 17*(3), 459-472.

Chamot, A. (1984). A transfer curriculum for teaching content-based ESL in the elementary school. In J. Handscome, R. Orem, & B. Taylor (Eds.), *On TESOL '83: The question of control.* Washington, DC: Teachers of English to Speakers of Other Languages.

Chastain, K. (1976). *Developing second language skills: Theory to practice.* Chicago: Rand McNally.

Christison, M., & Krahnke, K. (1986). Student perceptions of academic language study. *TESOL Quarterly, 20*(1), 61-82.

Corbett, S., & Flint Smith, W. (1984). Identifying student

learning styles: Proceed with caution. *Modern Language Journal, 68*(3), 212-221.

Corder, S. (1973). *Introducing applied linguistics.* Harmonsworth: Penguin.

Cummins, J. (1981). The role of primary language development in promoting success for language minority students. In Office of Bilingual Education (Ed.), *Schooling and language minority students: A theoretical framework.* Los Angeles: Evaluation, Dissemination, and Assessment Center, California State University.

DiPietro, R.J. (1982). The open-ended scenario: A new approach to conversation. *TESOL Quarterly, 16*(1), 15-20.

Dobson, J.M., & Sedwick, F. (1975). *Conversation in English: Points of departure.* New York: American Book Co.

Dubin, F., & E. Olshtain. (1986). *Course design: Developing programs and materials for language learning.* Cambridge: Cambridge University Press.

Dulay, H., & Burt, M. (1976). *The bilingual syntax measure: Technical handbook.* New York: Harcourt Brace Jovanovich.

Dulay, H., Burt, M., & Krashen, S. (1982). *Language two.* New York: Oxford University Press.

Ellis, R. (1986). *Understanding second language acquisition.* Oxford: Oxford University Press.

Finocchiaro, M., & Brumfit, C. (1983). *The functional-notional approach: From theory to practice.* Oxford: Oxford University Press.

Firth, J.R. (1957). *Papers in linguistics, 1934-1951.* London: Oxford University Press.

Gattegno, C. (1972). *Teaching foreign languages in schools: The Silent Way* (2nd ed.). New York: Educational Solutions.

Halliday, M.A.K. (1973). *Explorations in the functions of language.* London: Arnold.

Genesee, F., Polich, E., & Stanley, M. (1977). An experimental French immersion program at the secondary school level: 1969-1974. *Canadian Modern Language Review, 33,* 318-332.

Hartwell, P. (1985). Grammar, grammars, and the teaching of grammar. *College English, 47*(2), 105-127.

Higgs, T., & Clifford, R. (1982). The push toward communication. In T. Higgs (Ed.), *Curriculum, competence, and the foreign language teacher.* Skokie, IL: National Textbook.

Hymes, D. (1972). On communicative competence. In J.B. Pride & J. Holmes (Eds.), *Sociolinguistics.* Harmondsworth, Middlesex, England: Penguin Books.

Kelly, L.G. (1969). *25 centuries of language teaching.* Rowley, MA: Newbury House.

Krahnke, K.J. (1981). *Incorporating communicative instruction into academic preparation ESL curricula.* (ERIC Document Reproduction Service No. ED 210 915)

Krahnke, K.J., & Knowles, M. (1984). *The basis for belief: What ESL teachers believe about language teaching and why.* Paper presented at the 18th annual meeting of Teacher of English to Speakers of Other Languages, Houston, March, 1984.

Krashen, S. (1982). *Principles and practice in second language acquisition.* Oxford: Pergamon.

Krashen, S. (1985). *The input hypothesis: Issues and implications.* New York: Longman.

Krashen, S., & Terrell, T. (1983). *The natural approach: Language acquisition in the classroom.* San Francisco: Alemany Press.

Lambert, W., & Tucker, G.R. (1972). *The bilingual education of children.* Rowley, MA: Newbury House.

Lapkins, S., & Cummins, J. (1984). Canadian French immersion education: Current administrative and instructional practices. In California State Board of Education, *Studies in immersion education.* Sacramento, CA: Office of Bilingual Bicultural Education, California State Board of Education.

Littlewood, W. (1981). *Communicative language teaching.* Cambridge: Cambridge University Press.

Long, M., & Sato, C. (1983). Classroom foreigner talk discourse: Forms and functions of teachers' questions. In H. Seliger & M. Long (Eds.), *Classroom oriented research in second language acquisition.* Rowley, MA: Newbury House.

Lozano, F., & Sturtevant, J. (1981). *Life styles.* New York: Longman.

Mackey, W.F. (1965). *Language teaching analysis.* London: Longman.

Mason, C. (1971). The relevance of intensive training in English as a foreign language for university students. *Language Learning, 21*(2), 197-204.

McKay, S. (1980). Towards an integrated syllabus. In K. Croft (Ed.), *Reading in English as a second language.* Boston: Little-Brown.

Mohan, B. (1979). Relating language teaching and content teaching. *TESOL Quarterly, 13*(2), 171-182.

Munby, J. (1978). *Communicative syllabus design.* Cambridge: Cambridge University Press.

New English 900. New York: Collier Macmillan.

Paulston, C.B. (1974). Linguistic and communicative competence. *TESOL Quarterly, 8(4),* 347-362.

Plaister, T. (1976). *Developing listening comprehension for ESL students.* Englewood Cliffs, NJ: Prentice-Hall.

Richards, J., & Rodgers, T. (1982). Method: Approach, design, and procedure. *TESOL Quarterly, 16(2),* 153-168.

Rivers, W. (1981). *Teaching foreign-language skills.* Chicago: University of Chicago Press.

Steiner, R. (1975). Performing with objectives. Rowley, MA: Newbury House.

Swain, M. (1984). A review of immersion education in Canada research and evaluation studies. In California State Board of Education, *Studies in immersion education.* Sacramento, CA: Office of Bilingual Bicultural Education, California State Board of Education.

Tarone, E. (1986). Variability in interlanguage use: A study of style shifting in morphology and syntax. *Language Learning, 35(3),* 373-404.

U.S. Dept. of Health & Human Services. (1985). *Competency-Based Mainstream English Language Training Project (MELT)* (Resource Package). Washington, DC: Social Security Administration, Office of Refugee Resettlement.

van Ek, J.A. (1976). *The threshold level for modern language learning in schools.* London: Longman.

Widdowson, H. (1978). *Teaching language as communi-*

cation. Oxford: Oxford University Press.

Widdowson, H.G. (1979). *Explorations in applied linguistics.* Oxford: Oxford University Press.

Wilkins, D.A. (1976). *Notional syllabuses.* Oxford: Oxford University Press.

Wolfson, N., & Judd, E. (1983). *Sociolinguistics and language acquisition.* Rowley, MA: Newbury House.

Yalden, J. (1983). *The communicative syllabus: Evolution, design, and implementation.* Oxford: Pergamon.

Yorkey, R., Barrutia, R., Chamot, A., Rainey de Diaz, I., Gonzalez, J.B., Ney, J.B., & Woolf, W.L. (1984). *New intercom.* Boston: Heinle and Heinle.

About the Author

Karl J. Krahnke (Ph.D., The University of Michigan) is an Assistant Professor of English and Director of ESL Teacher Training at Colorado State University. He is the co-author, with Mary Ann Christison, of "Recent language research and some language teaching principles," published in the *TESOL Quarterly,* and numerous short articles and reviews. He has taught English as a second language and administered ESL programs in Afghanistan, Iran, Michigan, Washington, and Utah.